ROCK CLIMBING IN BRITAIN

ROCK CLIMBING IN BRITAIN

WILLOW BOOKS
Collins
8 Grafton Street, London W1
1984

Willow Books
William Collins & Sons plc
London · Glasgow · Sydney · Auckland · Toronto ·
Johannesburg

Front and back covers: Mick Lovatt on the Great White
(E7 6c), White Tower, Mother Carey's Kitchen,
Pembroke.

First published in Great Britain 1984
© David Jones 1984

Jones, David
Rockclimbing in Britain
1. Rockclimbing – Great Britain
1. Title
796.5'223'0941 GV199.44.G7

ISBN 0 00 218078 2

Filmset in Sabon by
Rowland Phototypesetting (London) Ltd
Printed and bound in Italy by
New Interlitho S.P.A.

I would like to thank everyone who contributed to the production of this book. To the people who gave me fantastic encouragement and assisted with the shooting: Phil Burke, Ed Cleasby, Nick Dixon, Ian Dunn, Phil Davidson, John Delamont, Rowland Edwards, Marion Evans, Ron and Gill Fawcett, Steve Findlay, Gary Gibson, Pat and Michael Godfrey, Rick Graham, Dennis Gleeson, Joe Healey, Dave Kirby, Daniel Lee, Gary Latter, Ian Lonsdale, Gerry and Margaret Lynch, Rob Matheson, Penny Melville, Andy Meyers, Guy Mclelland, John Monks, Steve Monks, Alan Murray, Elaine Nicholls, Chris Nicholson, Andy Pollitt, Jerry Peel, Ray Parker, Al Phizacklea, John Redhead, Gordon Stainforth, David Towse, Pete Whillance, Nigel Birtwell, Jerry Moffatt, Mark Lynden, Prizm Laboratory, Ron Bagley Laboratory.

To Anne Jones, John Delamont, Dill, Derek and Graeme Allen who gave me invaluable help and advice when writing the text and to Edilrid Ropes, Berghaus Scarpa, DMM, Wild Country and Clog for allowing me to test their equipment.

To all those who seconded the climbs:
Rowland Edwards(37), Mark Edwards(43), Alun Richardson(54,85), Nick Lander(22), Matt Saunders(17), Peter Hancock(19), Graeme Allen(27), Adam Hudson(58),
Judy Carroll(79), John Hartley(97), Mick Lovatt(50), Steve Monks(48), Duncan Critchley(59), Lydia Bradey(87), Dick Broomhead(51), Phil Biggs(77), Martin Veale(64), Dave Barrell(86), Mark Prettey (99), Ian Jones(83,52), Steve Andrews(93), Jim Ballard(32), John Allen(61,76), Chris Nicholson(78), Pat Littlejohn(60), Dave Armstrong(13), David Lang(31), Ian Fox(66), Malcolm Campbell(41), Janet Minot(3), Matthew Woodford(3), Nick Jones(67), Graham Dungate(67), Bob Chambers(67), Paul Linfoot(67), Simon Kennedy(67), Pete Varlow(67), Rob Kieschke(68), Dave Towse(75,100), Dave Lawson(70,30), Martin Crook(28), Paul Lee(8), Jules Taylor(80), Gerry Lynch(36), Phil Kelly(35), Paul Wood(74), Nigel Birtwell(57,95), Alan Murray(84), Penny Melville(15), Bob Utley(23), Ray Parker(26), Al Phizacklea(39,47,45,82), Rob Knight(14), Dave Kirby(9), Rick Graham(71), Gary Latter(65,98), Dave Cuthbertson(72), Frans Collignon(88), Ken Fryer(18), Kenny Simpson(6), David Hilley(4), Nipper Harrison(20) and Greg Forward(62).

Most of all, I would like to thank my parents for their marvellous support while I was shooting and writing this book, the photographic labs who processed my film faultlessly and, of course, the Cardiff and Manchester Weather Centres whose advice made this book possible.

DAVID JONES
London, 1984

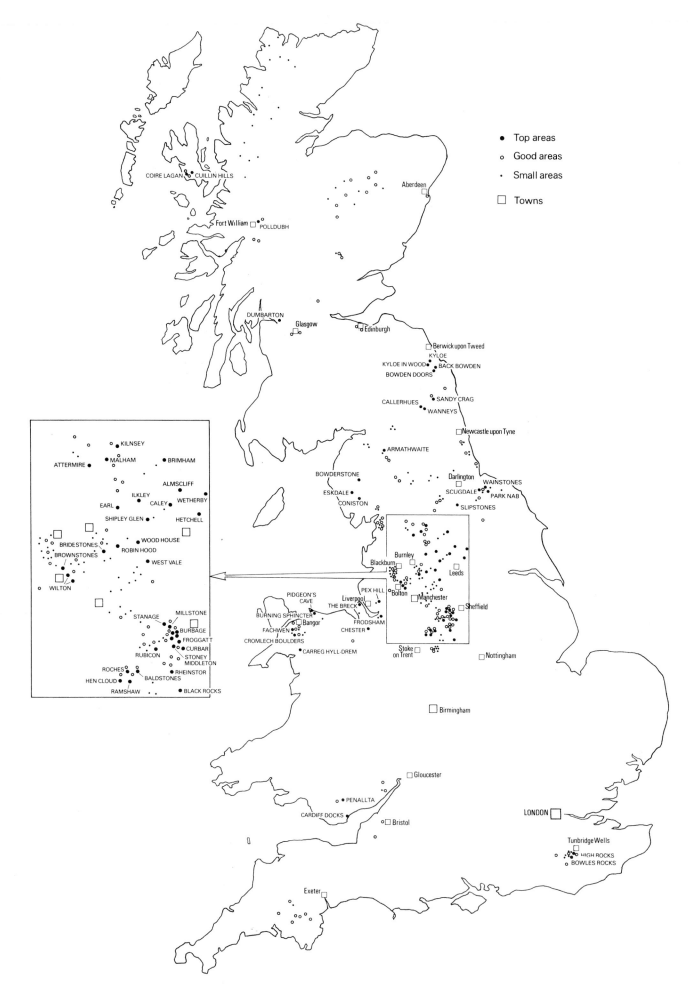

THE PRINCIPAL BOULDERING AREAS IN GREAT BRITAIN

▬ CONTENTS ▬

— INTRODUCTION —

At the age of 12, having always been one for fun and adventure, I found myself standing at the foot of a rockface in North Wales with my friend urging me on. I proceeded up into the wilderness above, only to be terrified for the duration of the climb. My friend followed me up and then we abseiled down which I enjoyed as I had done it a few times before in the scouts. Experience over and frozen – it was March – we set óff home. Lengthy discussions followed concerning the safety of the washing line we were using (not to be advised!) and the prospect of having to face an irate mother. However, on returning home we discovered that a new washing line had been bought which meant we could keep ours. Our enthusiasm fired, the washing line gave three years' service for climbing and abseiling and needless to say, no one ever fell off.

These were my first experiences of a sport which I sometimes enjoyed, sometimes not. However, the fact remained that I wanted to climb. No one forced me and I never felt I had to climb; it was something I did occasionally from self motivation only. To me this is the essence of rock climbing. There are no rules or necessary qualifications, no one to dictate what you must or must not do. If you don't feel in the mood or if the weather's awful, you can climb or you can stay at home. If you are not able to free climb a pitch then you can use equipment to aid your ascent. It is your decision. And if you wish to dispense with safeguards and solo a climb, it is your privilege to take that risk. A code of ethics exists in rock climbing which is adhered to by most. It has evolved over many years and reflects what are felt to be good and bad styles or methods of ascent. However, it is not a list of rules and the penalty for ignoring them cannot affect a climber's freedom to climb but only his reputation, which will be discussed by other climbers in the pub, café or gym.

Soloing is the purest form of rock climbing; the climber tackles an ascent equipped with nothing but a pair of boots and a chalkbag. The challenge is very real, because any lapse in concentration or lack of ability is likely to result in a fall, probably with serious consequences. However, soloing gives an unequalled feeling of isolation and independence. To me, soloing provides the greatest satisfaction and enjoyment in rock climbing and I attempt it only when I am in the right mood.

Leading (plus seconding) is the most common mode of climbing. One climber takes the role of leader and the other that of second. The leader ties the rope to his harness and sets off up the rockface. The leader places protection at intervals in the rock in the form of runners. Runners are wedge-shaped pieces of metal attached to sections of wire or cord. They are slotted into corresponding V-shaped parts of cracks or points of weakness in the rockface, and then connected to the climbing rope by metal snaplinks – karabiners – which are clipped on to the loops in the wire or cord and then to the rope itself. Having arranged a runner, the leader will continue his ascent. The other climber – the second – will pay out the rope via a braking device on his harness. If the leader should fall off, the second will lock the rope in the device to prevent any more being paid out; the leader will fall past his runner and stop. The distance he falls will

Joe Healey soloing Black Magic 6a at Pex Hill Quarry, Merseyside

be twice that between him and the runner; how far he is above it, plus the same distance below. The leader will place several runners on a climb, and will check that his last one is always nearer him than the ground.

If a climb is too long to be completed in a single lead, the leader will stop at one of his runners and attach himself directly to it. This is usually done where there is a ledge to stand or sit on, but if not, in the middle of a steep section. The leader, attached to the rock by the runner, forms what is known as a belay. The second now climbs, taking out the protection (runners) as he passes each placement, while the leader safeguards him by taking in the rope through the braking device on his harness. The second will carry on past the leader, becoming the new leader and continue to the next belay point or to the top: each section to be led is called a pitch. A leader requires many skills but the most important is the ability to place runners that will stop him falling should he come off. The second must also be competent and alert as it is up to him to protect the leader if he falls. They are totally reliant on each other.

Most cliffs in Britain have been climbed and most of the climbs have been documented. Pocket-sized guidebooks describe all the climbs in a particular area and also provide maps and illustrations. This means that climbers can prepare for the sort of problems they will encounter on a particular route, because these are described in detail, and also be guided by the grade. Grades categorise climbs according to their difficulty. Climbers will know from experience what grades they can manage and so are able to choose which ones to try from the guidebook. Over the past 100 years many climbs have been made and recorded. The first to lead a particular route has the privilege of naming it.

Obviously, climbing a new route is different from climbing an established one because there is no information about how hard it is, or how easy it will be to place protection. However, this is not true in practice because of the habit of making inspections and 'practice' ascents safe-guarded from above, plus the fact that a potential first ascensionist is likely to find out who has failed while attempting it before him and why. Sometimes the first ascensionist gives the climb a higher grade than he had to cope with when leading it, because whereas he had the benefit of prior inspection, the subsequent ascensionists are expected to climb the route 'on sight'.

The grading system used in climbing is, at present, a complete maze. It varies from area to area, different terms are used to describe similar climbs and the criteria used to assess the degree of difficulty is not uniform. Many anomalies exist between Britain and other countries where fixed protection points are more common and make climbing much safer. A grading in Britain must express not only technical difficulty (size and availability of holds) but also how sustained the difficulties are and how dangerous the climb.

Rock climbing can be practised virtually anywhere – quarries, sea cliffs, mountain crags, small outcrops – and is essentially a sport in its own right. The high-grade rock climber is interested in climbing one specific rockface only. His objective is a particular route up that rockface regardless of situation or locality, and his approach is that of the athlete. If the crag is in a valley high up in the Lake District, the climber will derive added enjoyment from the magnificent scenery, but normally he will be attracted by the quality of the climbing rather than the scenery. Other types of climber, of course, may have slightly different priorities: rock climbing at a more moderate standard is an important, and quite spicy ingredient in general mountaineering, and in this form it provides great pleasure for many people.

Rock climbing is made a varied sport by different regional characteristics but more importantly by the many different types of rock. Climbing on limestone is a totally different skill to climbing on granite, quartzite or gritstone. Each type of rock is completely individual and the limestone in one valley can be very different from that in the next. This makes a flexible

Alun Richardson leading Finger Print E3 6a at Ogmore, South Wales; he is clipping his rope into protection while hanging on with one arm

approach – to different frictional qualities, different types of protection placement, and so on – a constant necessity. On sea cliffs, the external dangers of incoming tides and rough seas present a constant hazard, occasionally necessitating some speedy climbing in order to avoid taking a dip.

The diversity of climbing in Britain makes it a climber's paradise. The climbs are neither as long as, for instance, in the Yosemite Valley in California, nor as well-protected as those in Europe but the urge to climb can be satisfied by the smaller crags which abound in routes of quality and interest and are scattered throughout the country. This book includes photographs of every major climbing area in Britain, and I have tried to recreate the immense variety and dramatic quality of the sport through the medium of the camera. It is a colourful, action-filled sport and I hope the results reveal, better than any words can, the reason why I want to go rock climbing in Britain.

▬ GRADING ▬

In Britain the technical grade generally reflects the difficulty of a particular move on rock. The grade takes the move into consideration only and is quite subjective since people of similar ability will usually prefer certain rock types and have different physiques that will find some moves easier than others. Most beginners find grades 1a to 4c within their capability, all moves being new yet none have really small holds. A quite athletic person with naturally strong fingers could probably manage a 5a move. At 5b the holds are about the size of cassette box edge, at 5c and 6a the edge of the cassette, at 6b & 6c the tape width. Thereafter the complexity of the move is increased, the angle of rock acuter and the holds slope downwards.

Britain's grading system takes into consideration the exposure and sustained nature of climbing, looseness of rock, and level of protectability which in turn is linked to the technically hardest move. This is because everyone usually has a limit to the difficulty of move they can physically achieve; the other factors can be overcome by skill and experience.

For example, E2 has the following levels of difficulty:
E2 5a to 5a moves high up, poor protection, dubious rock
E2 5b to 5b moves high up, poor protection
E2 5c to 5c moves with adequate protection
E2 6a to 6a moves near ground or very well protected

Grading in other countries usually measures the technical difficulty only and the comparative standards are shown, many overlapping because of grading subjectivity. If a route is unprotectable, an expansion bolt is usually drilled but in Britain this habit is strongly condemned since most climbs are protectable and those which are not should be top roped or soloed, with the exception of limestone.

This chart shows how the technical grades correspond with the overall grades in the British open-ended system. The higher grades cover a wider range of technical difficulty since climbs of Very Severe and above become increasingly strenuous and hard to protect.

	1a	1b	2a	2b	3a	3b	4a	4b	4c	5a	5b	5c	6a	6b	6c	7a	7b	
MOD	●●	●●								○○	○○	○○						E1
DIFF		●●	●●							○○	○○	○						E2
V.DIFF			●●	●●							○○	○○	○					E3
H.V.DIFF				●●	●●							○○	○○	○○				E4
MILD.S.					●●	●●							○	○○	○○			E5
SEVERE						●●	●●						○○	○○	○○	○		E6
H.SEVERE							●●	●●						○○	○○	○○	○	E7
VS.								●●	●●	●●				○	○○	○○	○○	E8
HVS.									●●	●●	●●			○○	○○	○○	○○	E9

■HISTORY■

The earliest recorded feat of rock climbing in Britain was in 1798 when Reverends William Bingley and Peter Williams climbed the east terrace of Clogwyn du'r Arddu, North Wales, in search of botanical specimens. An easy scramble by today's standards, they found it rather frightening with a few bad moments caused by loose rock. Only Williams had nails in his boots and had to help Bingley up at one point by unbuckling his belt and offering him the other end. Both reached the top and were able to carry their specimens home safely.

In the late eighteenth and early nineteenth centuries the fascination for Romantic landscapes – the exhilarating terror inspired by rushing waterfalls, craggy terrain and unattainable mountain peaks – resulted in a growing interest in and appreciation of mountain scenery in Britain and the Alps. Tourist guides and artists' impressions exaggerated the rugged, grand and formidable quality of the scenery, stressed the dangerous and forbidding nature of the mountain country and, in general, presented an image of awesome wildness which even in those less populated times must have been grossly exaggerated. One typical publication, the 1825 edition of Otley's *Guide to the Lakes*, contained a description of Pillar Rock in Ennerdale emphasising its precipitousness and pronouncing it 'unclimable'. This must have seemed quite amusing to the locals as there was an age-old tradition of scrambling on the fells, partly as a test of nerves and partly for more practical reasons such as the rescue of crag-fast sheep and the raiding of eagles' nests to stop them breeding. John Atkinson, a shepherd from Croftfoot, quickly disproved Otley's theory by climbing Pillar Rock in the summer of 1826. That the climb was repeated soon after by three more shepherds suggests that the local hill farmers were already very familiar with Pillar Rock and how to climb it. The Old West Route, the probable line of ascent, is not a rock climb by modern standards but the feat was of great interest and amazement to the readers of the local papers in the Lake District.

Rock climbing of various sorts had been done for centuries before it evolved as a sport, for both pleasure and everyday work. For instance, Scottish islanders would climb their sea cliffs in bare feet to steal eggs from seabirds' nests and would frequently scramble up climbs categorised as severe today. Quarrymen in Derbyshire and Dorset, miners in Cornwall and hill dwellers in the Lakes, Scotland and Snowdonia would all have been well used to scaling rocks. Consequently, the habit of claiming firsts seems a little pompous, especially in the case of the more obvious and easy routes. A great many of the easy ridge and gully climbs are likely to have been successfully negotiated long before they were recorded in hotel logbooks, if not by locals then by early fell walkers looking for short cuts and more adventurous ways up or down.

Pillar Rock was 'first ascended by an amateur' in 1848, when Lieutenant Wilson (RN) of Troutbeck climbed the Old West Route and left his name in a ginger-beer bottle on the summit. C.A.O. Baumgartner tried a different approach in 1850, and climbed the east and north sides to establish the 'Old Wall Route', also a scramble rather than a climb, but an early example of seeking a new and alternative line instead of being content with a single way to a summit. From that time onwards, the rock became the scene of ever more regular ascents. In 1875 the Reverend James Jackson proclaimed himself 'Patriarch of the Pillarites' after scaling it at the age of 79, by yet another scrambler's route, the Slab and Notch, pioneered in 1861. The old man used iron stakes to help himself up – perhaps the first-ever aid extravaganza. Jackson fell and was killed when attempting his third ascent of the rock, at the age of 82.

1850-80 were energetic days in the mountains and scrambling on the rocks became a popular pastime in Wales and the Lakes during this time.

Exploration of the Cuillin mountains in Scotland, most thoroughly by the famous Alexander Nicolson in the 1870s, had begun in 1836. But the most notable early rock climb was 'Ossian's Ladder', a route to Ossian's Cave in Glencoe established in 1868 by Neil Marquis, a local shepherd. Graded Mild Difficult today and 200 feet long, it may have been inspired by romantic and patriotic feelings – the 'Ossian Craze' was part of the Victorian nostalgia for a more heroic age. Glencoe, though, remained inaccessible and no other significant climb was recorded until 1894.

William Cecil Slingsby was a formidable mountaineer and one of the best rock climbers of his time. As early as 1864 he and his circle of friends were using Crookrise Rocks in Yorkshire as a climbing area. They taught themselves to climb here and at Almscliff during the 1860s and 1870s and, though few records survive, it is likely that all the easy routes and perhaps some not so easy, were first attempted during this period. Slingsby became a prominent member of the Alpine Club but remained loyal to the cause of rock climbing at a time when many British Alpinists looked on the new sport with disdain. He came to be regarded as the father figure of rock climbing and also father-in-law to Geoffrey Winthrop Young. Although mostly remembered for his mountaineering and for pioneering the development of skiing in Norway, there seems little doubt that he enjoyed rock climbing for its own sake, and his influence must have been considerable. Among his many first ascents was Slingsby's Chimney on Scafell.

Perhaps the first mountain rock climb in Britain recognisably modern in concept and quality is the east ridge of the Inaccessible Pinnacle on Skye (Difficult, 150 feet) climbed in 1880 by the Pilkington brothers. There is no easier way to the pinnacle, the true summit of Sgurr Dearg, so the route can be seen more as an example of mountaineering than rock climbing but it remains an interesting and worth-while excursion. Apart from this, rock climbing development in the early 1880s, is largely the story of two individuals exploring independently of each other: A. H. Stocker in Wales and W. P. Haskett Smith in the Lakes.

At Wasdale in 1881, Haskett Smith met F. H. Bowring, a climber who liked to keep off the beaten track. Bowring had had some experience of exploring gullies, and introduced Haskett Smith to the delights of scrambling. Haskett Smith was quick to adopt the pastime himself. He visited Great End Crag, Bowfell Buttress, Pavey Ark, Gimmer Crag, and Pillar Rock, climbing mostly in promising looking gullies, discovering routes of Moderate to Difficult standard of anything from 50 to 600 feet.

In 1883 A. H. Stocker and T. W. Wall made the first ascent of the huge West Buttress at Lliwedd in Wales by a route which is difficult to reconstruct from their description, but obviously some variant on the Bilberry Terrace climbs. Stocker's and Wall's route is graded Moderate in perfect conditions but as their attempt took place in early January, the climb was probably considerably more severe than this suggests. In April 1884, Stocker returned with A. G. Parker, and climbed what is now known as the Primitive Route (Difficult, 1000 feet), on this occasion documenting their climb rather more accurately. He climbed in other areas as well, and recorded his ascent of the Parson's Nose Route (Difficult, 250 feet).

In the same year Haskett Smith climbed the classic Needle Ridge with John Robinson (Difficult, 325 feet) on the Napes cliffs of Great Gable. They did not yet use ropes and Haskett Smith admitted that they undertook the climb rather timidly, avoiding difficulties wherever possible. But two precedents had been established during this period: the challenge of climbing a particular rockface as an end in itself rather than as part of a route to a summit and the practice of making a complete record of any new climb discovered. These two aims traditionally define the difference between rock climbing and mountaineering in general.

In 1886 Haskett Smith climbed Napes Needle (Hard Very Difficult, 55 feet) and many books generally agree that this marked the beginning of 'the sport of rock climbing'. Although this is not quite accurate, the Needle photographed well, and the spectacle of climbers on its tip was a dramatic sight which came to symbolise the essence of the new sport. The importance of this climb has been overvalued at the expense of other achievements of the same period or earlier, but it was a solo ascent at a very respectable grade, and undoubtedly a rock climb and nothing else. Even though the difference then between leading and soloing was not so great as it is today, the psychological pressure of making such a climb – with no guarantee that the topmost part of the pinnacle was firm or that the moves leading up to it could easily be made or reversed – would have been considerable and it is justifiably still considered a breakthrough. In the same year Stocker and Parker were active on Skye, where they climbed the other famous route of the same kind – the short, western arête of the Inaccessible Pinnacle (Very Difficult, 40 feet) – a major landmark on the traverse of the Cuillin Ridge.

Although the period 1880-1900 is often described as 'the gully era', 'the gully and ridge era' would be more accurate. Haskett Smith was keep to explore gullies and many difficult ones were tackled in the 1890s and early 1900s, but plenty of ridge climbs were also being made during the same decades. In addition to their Inaccessible Pinnacle climb, the Pilkingtons ascended the Pinnacle Ridge, Sgurr nan Gillean (Difficult) in 1880; the next route on Lliwedd, Eckenstein and Scully's Central Gully and West Peak (Difficult, 1000 feet, 1887) is mostly an exercise in ridge following as were the first two; Slingsby and friends added Slingsby's Route (Severe, 400 feet) to Sgurr nan Gillean in 1890; and the first major route by the later celebrated Owen Glynne Jones, the Cyfrwy Arête on Cader Idris (Difficult, 500 feet, 1888) is also of this type. There is a common misconception that climbers begun by exploring gullies and ventured on to steep open rock only when they had developed greater confidence but, in fact, easy scrambles on gullies and ridges were equally pursued. Haskett Smith preferred gully climbing, not because he was scared of more open terrain, but because the route was already defined. Most ridge and gully climbers of this era considered the steeper and more exposed walls between the ridges and gullies to be dangerous, 'unjustifiable' places to climb.

In 1890 the Peak District began to be explored in earnest. J. W. Puttrell and friends began to investigate Cratcliffe Tor, the Black Rocks of Cromford, and the Edges of Stanage, Froggatt, and Gardom's. All are now among the most frequented outcrops in the country. Technical standards rose sharply, with Hermitage Crack (Hard Severe) at Cratcliffe probably Puttrell's finest achievement at that time.

1892 found Godfrey Solly, Slingsby, G. Baker and W. Brigg at Wasdale. Solly led the first ascent of Eagle's Nest Ridge Direct on the Napes, Great Gable. This climb, a Mild Very Severe, was an exceptional lead and a new departure in technical ability. The severity of the climb worried Solly and Slingsby sufficiently to wonder whether or not it was best left unrecorded, in case someone died attempting to repeat it. Owen Glynne Jones later climbed the route and survived, but was also impressed: 'that almost vertical buttress looks impossible, and to nearly everybody it is so,' he wrote. 'The fact is that the ridge is not to be recommended.'

Jones was a tremendously keen climber and Alpinist. He was living in Kensington and studying engineering when he made his ascent of the Cyfrwy Arête poorly equipped and alone. The latter half of 1890s were the great years of his partnership with the Abraham brothers: they made many impressive climbs together in Snowdonia and the Lake District. Two of the most remarkable were Jones's 1896 route to the Scafell Pinnacle from Deep Ghyll and Kern Knotts Crack in 1897. The route from Deep Ghyll is graded Mild Severe, but its importance does not so much lie in its technical achievement as its nature: it was of the kind traditionally considered dangerous and unjustifiable as it followed a sinuous groove up one of the most intimidating faces leading to the pinnacle. Many disapproved, saying that Jones, who had a reputation for being reckless, was likely to bring the sport into disrepute. Because of his shortsightedness, he was largely unaffected by exposed situations. In his *Rock Climbing in the English Lake District*, Jones modestly confessed that he and the Abrahams had become lost while attempting the Hopkinsons' more indirect climb to the pinnacle, made in 1893, which seems likely enough. In any case the route was completed and there is an honourable tradition of pioneering by mistake in British rock climbing.

There was neither mistake nor recklessness in his ascent of Kern Knotts Crack in 1897. Showing a remarkable appreciation of the potential hazards of climbing for his time, he had the good sense to top rope the crack twice before leading it. It was the second of the Lake District's Mild Very Severes, so this proved to be a wise precaution, which brought much scorn from others who regarded such methods of pioneering as unfair. None offered to lead the crack on sight, however, not even the formidable Edward 'Aleister' Crowley, who later became notorious as 'the wickedest man in the world' because of his career as an occultist. Crowley appears to have climbed a great deal in the Lake District, and to a very high standard, but his only route still on record is a variation on the original Napes Needle climb, one of several added over the years.

Jones died in an accident in the Alps in 1899, having established a number of important climbs in the intervening years: the 'C' Gully on Wasdale Screes (Mild Very Severe), a second route to the Scafell Pinnacle this time from Lords Rake (Severe), and Walker's Gully on Pillar Rock (Hard Severe). It is interesting to note that he is one of the first climbers to have recognised the importance of training and he practised with weights whenever his work kept him in London.

Around the turn of the century, J. W. Puttrell, who had by then also met the Abraham brothers and climbed with them in the Lake District, began a new phase of pioneering in the Peaks. He was the first to venture on to the area's limestone crags, climbing a number of routes at Harborough and Rainster Rocks. These outcrops, however, were unique and more significant was his lead of Dargai Crack (Mild Very Severe) at Cave Dale, an extremely difficult route on a type of rock that many were still dismissing as unsuitable for free climbing 50 years later. He did not neglect his beloved gritstone edges either, and in 1900 led his fierce *Coup de Main* climb, the Downfall Groove at Kinder Downfall. This climb, Hard Very Severe, remained the most difficult in Britain for many years to come though few recognised it then.

Outcrop training was beginning to assume great importance, and the gritstone edges of the Peak District and Yorkshire were proving themselves invaluable nurseries for aspiring cragsmen. Virtually all notable climbers since then have had at least some opportunity to develop their skill on these crags. In 1900 the notable figure was Fred Botterill who, with W. Parsons, was using Almscliff as his practice ground.

During the early 1900s, few new areas received any significant attention with two main exceptions: Cornwall and Northumberland. Cornwall was the home of A. W. Andrews, a very active member of the early climbing fraternity who, with his sister, explored the Bosigran area and found the 700 feet Bosigran Ridge, a popular classic today. They climbed dressed in seaside clothes and tennis shoes. Andrews often invited his friends to stay, and these included some of the most famous climbers of the time, but surprisingly little climbing was done: perhaps because of the excellent weather and holiday atmosphere!

However, Winthrop Young and George Mallory managed to combine both interests in 1912, while making the first recorded climb at Carn Lês Boel, the Pinnacle Traverse, one scorching hot summer's day. They climbed in tennis shoes and dispensed with clothes altogether: the Penwith coast was lonelier then! Winthrop Young was also the most famous climber to climb in Northumberland, discovering that the crags of Simonside and Great Wanney were laced with many routes in the easier grades.

Back in the Lakes, C. W. Barton's Savage Gully (Mild Very Severe) and R. W. Broadrick's Broadrick's Crack (Hard Severe) on Pillar Rock and Dow Crag respectively, were acquiring fierce reputations. The Crack was the last of this trilogy of fine routes on Dow from the Broadrick brothers, while Savage Gully was the 'last great problem' of the time.

In 1903 Fred Botterill established the route for which he is justly famed: Botterill's Slab on Scafell, climbed on sight in nailed boots, Lakeland's first full Very Severe and a frightening lead above a long drop. Even today, with all the additional comfort that a full rack of runners can provide, many find this climb intimidating. Botterill, of course, had no such safeguards. He took an ice axe to help clear the vegetation off the holds, but dropped it, perhaps fortunately.

Sadly in the same year R. W. Broadrick and his three companions were killed in an accident on Scafell. They were attempting a route on the pinnacle face climbed several years later by Herford and Sansom and they were all moving together, Alpine-style, tied to the rope at various points. The science of safe rope management was a difficult skill even among the climbers who were sensible enough to study the problems involved. Many, amazingly enough, gave the matter little thought. This was the first major climbing tragedy in the Lakes. The first man to propose that the climber belaying his companion should anchor himself to the rock, in anything like the modern method, was Claude Benson in 1909, and the technique was not universally adopted even then.

In Wales, the circle of climbers presided over by J. M. Archer Thomson was now very active in the Ogwen Valley and on Lliwedd. The first route on Lliwedd's steeper east buttress was recorded in 1903: Route 1 (Hard Difficult, 295 feet), the work of Thomson and Eckenstein. Others were soon added. The Abraham brothers, though deeply affected by the death of Jones, continued to climb and pioneered in Scotland, Wales and the Lakes. Cousin's Buttress (Severe) on Ben Nevis, climbed by C. and H. Walker in 1904, continued the trend initiated by Norman Collie and his companions ten years earlier to develop many of the big Scottish cliffs and produce routes of the same technical standard as those achieved elsewhere. But Scotland with its small climbing population, severe weather, big, remote mountains and huge areas of untouched rock was already settling into a pattern of exploration more geared towards mountaineering than specialised rock climbing. Given the circumstances this was understandable, and illustrates the difference between the comparatively compact and accessible climbing areas of Snowdonia and the Lakes with those typical of the Highlands. Consequently, the Scots developed their winter ice climbing to a much higher degree technically than their expertise on rock.

The Abraham brothers had never seen eye to eye with Archer Thomson who disliked their boisterous manner and the way in which they were benefiting financially from selling books and photographs on climbing. Thomson felt that any degree of publicity would be harmful to the sport, feeling that 'the spirit of the hills' could be appreciated only by well-bred gentlefolk. The Abrahams, for their part, are likely to have found Thomson aloof and snobbish, and it probably did little to improve relations between them when the brothers climbed Lliwedd's Far East Cracks in 1905, at Hard Severe a new standard of difficulty for the cliff. In 1907 they were in Skye, and were led by H. Harland up the Direct Route to the Cioch. This is a tremendous climb on open rock, also at Hard Severe standard, giving good value for its grade.

A year later, George Mallory was active on Lliwedd, but climbed nothing so impressive as Mallory's Right Hand route (Mild Very Severe) on Gable Crag, Great Gable. This was also the year in which Harrison's Rocks at Tunbridge Wells were first noted by a climber, Charles Nettleton, who visited them with a friend then, but it is not known whether they did any climbing.

Puttrell continued to explore in the Peak District and was active at Froggatt Edge, also making further tentative forays on to the limestone crags when he visited High Tor and climbed Slanting Crack. Not a significant climb in itself, it was proof of Puttrell's interest in the possibilities of climbing limestone at a time when others regarded it with a mixture of righteous indignation and total ignorance. One of Puttrell's problems with the gritstone edges was that they formed parts of large estates patrolled by gamekeepers, most of whom were hostile to climbers. Consequently, climbing activity was restricted more by how easy it was to trespass undetected than by lack of enthusiasm or ability. Many of these crags did not become easily accessible until after the Second World War.

Development was now accelerating and becoming more widespread. Virtually all the interesting high mountains and cliffs in England and Wales had at least been visited, and most had been climbed. In Scotland the situation was rather different, but all the most likely areas had been investigated to some extent. South of the Border, low-lying crags in the mountain areas were receiving more attention. Clogwyn y Bustach, in the Nantgwynant valley, saw the addition of Lockwood's Chimney (Difficult), and though not hard it was unusual in that there is a tradition attached, which holds that it should be climbed by moonlight, in the worst possible conditions, by a large party of (preferably large) men. There was a surge of climbing activity during these years, abuptly curtailed by the outbreak of the First World War. The prominent figures were E. W. Steeple and Guy Barlow, who climbed extensively in the Cuillins of Skye adding the classic Grooved Arête climb to the east face of Tryfan, and Siegfried Herford and George Sansom. Herford was another climber who put training on Peak District gritstone to good use and he and Sansom are famous for their epic ascent of Scafell's Central Buttress, still graded Hard Very Severe but not climbed free until 1931; they used a complicated and precarious form of direct aid to surmount the crux pitch. It was, nevertheless, a daring and remarkable effort and they are also remembered for many other fine climbs in Wales and the Lakes. Herford also teamed up with George Mallory and Geoffrey Winthrop Young to make another epic foray, this time to the cliffs of Lliwedd where they completed a double traverse of the main buttresses in very fast time. This expedition is discouraged nowadays, due to the risk to others below from dislodged loose rock but then it was a fine demonstration of the talents of some of the country's best climbers. Herford, following Puttrell's example, was also responsible for an early climb on the limestone cliffs of the Peak District.

Many rudimentary guidebooks were published in 1913, covering various outcrops and crags now among the most famous in the country: Helsby, Hen Cloud and the Roches, the Kinder Scout area, the Black Rocks of Cromford. But the War halted any immediate further development and many leading climbers were killed in action to say nothing of those who had died in mountain accidents in the preceding years, such as Humphrey Owen Jones and the very talented Hugh Rose Pope. Herford was the most celebrated climber among the war casualties. Winthrop Young survived the War but lost a leg while serving in France with an ambulance unit. He came to be regarded as the father figure of the 1920s' and 1930s' Snowdonia climbers, as J. M. Archer Thomson had been before him; but, although he made great efforts to overcome his disability and continue climbing, his days as a cragsman were over and he was much affected by the loss of so many of his climbing friends. Mallory also survived the War, and continued to climb enthusiastically until his death on Everest in 1924. The Abraham brothers remained active but were now, of course, considerably older and they pioneered no more important climbs.

The gap in the ranks caused by the First World War was filled by a new generation of climbers, again benefiting from the now almost essential early training on gritstone. H. M. Kelly, an early champion of the use of rubber-soled footwear, made the first of the harder interwar climbs, Sodom and Gomorrah (both Very Severe) on Pillar Rock. George Bower, an engineer, also began to climb to a very high standard. He advocated the adoption of the shoulder belay, and the use of light Alpine line to reduce rope drag, and his widely-adopted technical innovations remained in use until the introduction of nylon ropes and karabiners after the Second World War. Equally able, though less prolific, was J. I. Roper. He and Bower added Great Central Route (Very Severe) to Dow Crag, and in 1920 it was Roper who made a major breakthrough. This was the Black Wall climb on Dow Crag (Hard Very Severe), led by Roper after several top rope inspections by the best climbers in the Lakes at the time, including himself, Bower, and Arthur Wakefield. In many respects it was the most formidable feat of climbing yet achieved: an unprotected lead of 120 feet at a technical standard approached only twice before. Bower made the second ascent a week later.

Bower pioneered extensively at this time, making first ascents on Pavey Ark, Gimmer Crag, Esk Buttress, Dow Crag, and in the Peak District. At the Ravenstones in the Chew Valley, he climbed Wedgwood Crack (Very Severe). In 1922 H. S. Gross climbed Eliminates 'B' and 'C' (both Very Severe) on Dow Crag. Despite advances in understanding the most effective use of available equipment, the interwar period must be regarded as the boldest in the history of British climbing, the earlier 'combined tactics' were no longer considered ethical, and many routes of varying grades were established which were made all the more formidable by the absence of adequate safeguards. The safety margins were exceeded time and again, yet some climbers seemed happy to perform regularly under these conditions at full Very Severe standard and occasionally above. The early successes of Bower, Roper, Kelly, Gross, and others were only the beginning of an enthusiastic trend towards difficult free climbing despite the considerable dangers.

In the Peak District Fred Pigott climbed Giant's Staircase (Very Severe) at Cratcliffe Tor, and Morley Wood climbed Priscilla Ridge (also Very Severe) at Laddow Rocks, to name only two among their many innovations. Gross completed his series of Eliminates on Dow Crag with Eliminate 'A' in 1923, the hardest and probably the finest. Major crags in the south west were explored in the same year, with Alison Rib being added at Bosigran, the 1923 route at Zennor, and Wogs (Difficult), the first recorded climb at Chudleigh Rocks. In the Lakes, H. M. Kelly climbed Tophet Wall (Severe) on Great Gable, and Appian Way (Severe) on Pillar Rock, both famous classics today. The hectic pace of development on the gritstone outcrops in Yorkshire and the Peak District was mainly because they were used as practice grounds by the best climbers of the day: additions were made at Dovestones, Stanage and Cromford Black Rocks, notably by Bower, Pigott, Kelly, and Fergus Graham.

In 1925 Graham climbed Holly Tree Wall (Very Severe) on Cwm Idwal and Moss Ledge Direct (Very Severe) on Scafell, perhaps the most remarkable of his many routes, often undertaken solo; he was probably the most able slab climber of the period. At Stanage, Kelly climbed the overhang to the left of Inaccessible Slab, Kelly's Overhang (Hard Very Severe, 5b), the hardest route on gritstone and possibly in Britain at the time. The first serious climbing on south-eastern sandstone began in 1926 and was pioneered by Nea and Jean Morin, Eric Shipton, Gilbert Peaker, Osbert Barnard, E. H. Marriott and Miss Marples. Harrison's Rocks was the centre of attention, and many of the cracklines were first ascended then.

1928 proved to be a full year, mainly due to the arrival on the scene of Colin Kirkus, Jack Longland, and Eric Byne. Fred Pigott had established the first important route on Clogwyn du'r Arddu, Pigott's Climb (Very Severe) in 1927 which Longland followed up with Longland's Slab (Very Severe). Attention was thus called to Wales's grandest cliff, the scene of the first documented rock climb 130 years earlier, but ignored by the early generations of climbers because of its exceptionally steep and intimidating character, which was emphasised by its grim, north-facing aspect. Kelly and Graham continued their explorations in the Lake District, but the classic ascent of the year was The Crack on Gimmer Crag (Mild Very Severe), climbed by A. B. Reynolds and G. G. Macphee, which is a steep, bold route and then heavily overgrown with vegetation. Reynolds made a habit of climbing barefoot, even in winter. Today The Crack is regarded as one of the best climbs in Cumbria, though most climbers prefer to use rock boots when tackling it! At Helsby, 11 Very Severes were added, 7 by Kirkus and 4 by F. E. Hicks. In the Peak District, Eric Byne rediscovered Birchen's and Chatsworth Edges.

In 1929 Alf Bridge straightened out a route made at Black Rocks by Longland the previous year, Birch Tree Wall (Very Severe). Birch Tree Direct is the true classic; a climb of character which is surprisingly bigger than it looks, and graced with an unexpected and exciting finish even by today's sophisticated standards. A string of Very Severes were added at Laddow Rocks: Tower Arête, Blacksmith, and Terrace Wall. But Longland was responsible for the next major step forward when at Idwal in 1930, he was leading Javelin Buttress and wandered off-route, continuing up an alternative line. He found one move particularly strenuous, but he was a fine athlete and possessed great finger strength, so thought little of it. The route he had established was Javelin Blade, Britain's first Extremely Severe, though no one realised how hard it was at the time. Its current guidebook grade is E1 5b and nothing as difficult was climbed for at least another eight years, and nothing harder for fifteen.

Deer Bield Crack in the Lake District (Hard Very Severe) on Deer Bield Buttress was of similar significance, a fierce undertaking which remained beyond the abilities of all but a few for many years. The man responsible was A. T. Hargreaves, a powerful and keen climber who left a superb legacy of rock climbs, none finer than this one. Colin Kirkus in Wales, having already pioneered a number of difficult ascents, such as Lot's Groove (Very Severe) on Glyder Fach, added Great Slab (Very Severe) to Clogwyn du'r Arddu, and the Nose Direct (Very Severe) to Dinas Mot. Both are magnificent, classic routes. In the Peak District Frank Elliott demonstrated his extraordinary ability by climbing Elliott's Eliminate, Wall End Slab Direct and many other hard problems at Stanage and elsewhere.

In the Llanberis Pass in 1931, John Menlove Edwards began exploring Dinas Cromlech, perhaps the most imposing cliff in Wales. He put up Spiral Stairs (Very Difficult) and Flying Buttress (Difficult) which are both characterised by a degree of exposure rarely equalled by other climbs at these grades. But his *tour de force* that year was his first free ascent of the Central Buttress route on Scafell (Hard Very Severe) climbed on sight in plimsolls. These undoubtedly helped him to succeed where Herford and Sansom had resorted to aid, but he later returned to claim the next free lead wearing nailed boots. Edwards possessed extraordinary physical strength, and made short work of the strenuous layback moves. Kirkus also visited Scafell, and climbed Mickledore Grooves (Very Severe). In 1932 Kirkus was back at Clogwyn du'r Arddu, and put up Curving Crack (Very Severe) in the company of a distinguished team including Alf Bridge, Maurice Linnell, and A. B. Hargreaves. The ascent of Curving Crack, another of Wales's great classics, followed on from Kirkus's activity on the cliff in the previous year, when Pedestal Crack (Very Severe) and Chimney Route (Very Severe) had been established.

1933 was Linnell's year on Clogwyn du'r Arddu. He climbed Overhanging Wall (Very Severe) and would probably have pioneered further but was killed in an accident on Ben Nevis the following winter. At Cratcliffe Tor Frank Elliott added Elliott's Unconquerable (Hard Very Severe) a desperate climb in its day. Elliott made a remarkable first ascent in 1934, when he tackled the great limestone walls at Stoney Middleton. The result, Aurora (Very Severe), was as impressive an innovation as Puttrell's early experiments. The general opinion was still that limestone was dangerous and unsuitable for free climbing, and this attitude was slow to change, but Elliott had done much to change it. Aurora is the first route on limestone, modern in approach, and Stoney Middleton is one of the most important climbers' cliffs in Britain.

Again in 1934, the first guidebook to Harrison's Rocks was published. It described some routes, such as Unclimbed Wall, which were undoubtedly then the most difficult technical problems in the country. In 1935 Cox and Hodgkin visited the Dewerstone in Devon and climbed two routes, including the very impressive Climber's Club Direct (Hard Very Severe). A scandal occurred in Snowdonia in 1936, when Teufel, Seldmayr and Jenkins put up the Munich Climb on Tryfan. The German Alpinists saw nothing wrong in using a piton for aid but the local climbers felt differently, and Edwards promptly freed the route of the offending ironmongery to give a Very Severe climb of quality but no great severity even by the existing standards. According to the then current climbing ethics it was unheard of to use a piton even for protection.

Three very significant hard climbs were put up in 1938. Diagonal on Dinas Mot (Hard Very Severe) was the finest of Birtwistle's many good routes. Another gritstone trainee, Birtwistle's climb is one of the greatest classics in Snowdonia and is in a serious situation requiring excellent balance. Edwards, partnered by F. J. R. Dodd, climbed Central Gully Direct at Lliwedd, the hardest of many lines he added while preparing a new edition of the Lliwedd guidebook. Edwards led the first pitch and Dodd the rest; the most recent guide to Lliwedd gives the grade as Hard Very Severe, and denies a higher rating than this to any of the other routes on the cliff, but it might be more realistic to regard the climb as Britain's second Extremely Severe. It was repeated 3 times in the next 15 years only. Finally, Jim Birkett climbed May Day Climb (Hard Very Severe) on Scafell in the Lake District, an outstanding achievement and the first of many major routes pioneered by this great cragsman.

The Second World War affected climbing activity less than might be expected. Edwards, a conscientious objector, was leading a reclusive lifestyle in North Wales and continued to climb energetically when not writing about some of his psychiatric theories. A remarkable number of new routes were pioneered in the early years of the war.

In Scotland, the redoubtable Dr J. H. B. Bell, whose performance seemed to improve with age, made many impressive climbs. The most influential in raising climbing standards was his Tough Brown Ridge Direct at Lochnagar, climbed with Miss N. Forsyth. This is graded Very Severe for a pitch which was considered fierce at the time, and is still regarded as more demanding than any on the early face routes made by the next generation of Cairngorms climbers. In Yorkshire, the remarkable Arthur Dolphin began his climbing career at Caley and Almscliff; various climbers were developing the crags of Northumberland throughout the 1940s; and Frank Elliott, by then living in London, turned his attention to another of the south-eastern sandstone outcrops, Eridge Green Rocks, where he climbed some exceptionally fierce new routes, notably Battlement Crack and Barbican Buttress. In the Lake District, a series of classic routes all of Very Severe standard were established by Bill Peascod; and Birkett added Tophet Grooves (Hard Very Severe) to the Napes, Great Gable.

Activity tailed off towards the end of the War and little of note was accomplished. But soon after the end of the War a route was made in North Wales that was as important a breakthrough as Longland's ascent of Javelin Blade. This was Suicide Wall Route 1, climbed in October 1945 by Chris Preston. Not only was it Extremely Severe but it is now graded E2 5c and was for several years afterwards the most difficult rock climb ever made in Britain. Edwards and Kirkus (the latter was killed while serving with the RAF in 1942) had both tried the climb and failed: it was beyond even their capabilities. Preston made an inspection by abseil before attempting to lead and his style of leading was identical to that used while pioneering the Black Wall Climb 25 years earlier. He led the crux pitch but was forced to ask for a top rope when his second found himself unable to follow; Preston had insufficient rope to continue to the top in one run-out. He returned with a strong party and completed the climb on 7 October. Little is known about Preston who climbed practically nothing else of note; he was a very fit and strong army officer and obviously with nerves of steel. Even the young Joe Brown, who romped up most of the previous generation's hard climbs a few years later, took some time to summon up the courage to make a repeat ascent, and he took care to improvise some running belays, having surveyed the route previously on a top rope. It was first soloed by Alan Rouse in 1970.

One unlikely consequence of the Second World War was that a great deal of specialised equipment found its way into the surplus stores. Among these items were many for which climbers could find a use and in particular: pitons, karabiners, and nylon rope. Nylon ropes were a new invention, stronger than hemp and extremely light. The effect of this equipment on climbing was mixed; there were good and bad points. The disadvantage of the piton was that it was inevitably used for direct aid as well as protection, and the honourable tradition of free climbing began to be compromised in a way that was not halted until the mid-1960s. The advantage, however, of the new equipment was that it provided a great opportunity to develop unprecedentedly high standards without involving suicidal levels of risk. The way was open to take steps towards creating the more gymnastic and aesthetic forms of free climbing found today.

In 1947 Johnny Cunningham climbed The Gallows (E1 5b) on the Buachaille Etive Mor. Here was a Scottish climber concerned with the possibilities of hard free climbing, and keen to see that proper emphasis was placed on its development north of the Border. This route was as hard as any in Britain with only one exception, Suicide Wall, and harder than most English and Welsh climbs still considered desperate at the time. Together with his fellow members in the Creagh Dhu club, Cunningham pioneered many difficult climbs in the late 1940s, following the trend started by Glasgow climbers and most notably Jock Nimlin in the 1930s. In 1949, Jim Birkett established Harlot Face (Hard Very Severe, 5a) on the Castle Rock of Triermain, to give the hardest lead in the Lake District. This was also the year in which the young Joe Brown began to climb seriously. He climbed the Right Unconquerable at Stanage Edge (Hard Very Severe, 5a) which was not as hard as its companion route, the Left Unconquerable (E1 5c) first

Joe Brown *Ken Wilson*

ascended that same year by Probert and Shutt, but probably finer and destined to become famous.

The partnership between Joe Brown and Don Whillans began in 1951. Throughout the 1950s they were the driving force behind the establishment of hard new routes in Wales and the Peak District. On Clogwyn du'r Arddu, Brown put up Diglyph (Hard Very Severe), Vember (E1) and The Boulder (Hard Very Severe). He and Whillans added Cemetery Gates (Hard Very Severe, 5a) on Dinas Cromlech, one of Britain's most famous rock climbs, and at Curbar Edge Brown climbed the Right Eliminate, thus creating a new 'hardest route on gritstone'. In 1952 Whillans made an assault on the great overhang at the Roches, establishing Sloth (Hard Very Severe), the main problem of which was not so much technique as approach: few would have possessed the fierce determination even to try. In the Lake District Harold Drasdo produced his Classic North Crag Eliminate (E1 5b) and Arthur Dolphin in magnificent form added Pegasus (Hard Very Severe) and Hell's Groove (E1) to Scafell's East Buttress. They were the best of a series of classic Lakeland climbs, including most notably the famous Kipling Groove (Hard Very Severe, 5a) on Gimmer Crag, which was climbed in 1948.

Two ascents made in Snowdonia in 1952 stand as milestones in the development of hard climbing. One is John Streetly's Bloody Slab (E2 5b) on the West Buttress of Clogwyn du'r Arddu, almost the hardest route in Wales at the time, and all the more astounding to contemporary climbers because Streetly, from Cambridge, was unknown to them: the other is, of course, Cenotaph Corner on Dinas Cromlech, probably the most famous of all British rock climbs. On the first attempt, Brown was placing a peg at the crux section near the top of the corner when he accidentally dropped his piton hammer which hit his second, Wilf White, on the head. He abandoned his perch immediately and roped down to see if White was injured only to be told to go back up and finish the climb! However, Brown needed more pegs to arrange some protection, so the attempt was postponed. He returned with Doug Belshaw and this time was more successful. Today this route is the most popular Extremely Severe in Britain: some would dispute its quality, but never its direct, magnificent line.

In 1953, Brown and Whillans were climbing again in North Wales including Clogwyn du'r Arddu. Dolphin put up Communist Convert on Raven Crag in the Lake District, so named because it runs from left to right up the crag. Sadly, Dolphin died in the Alps shortly afterwards and Britain lost one of its most talented climbers.

In the Peak District, another leap forward in leading standards was made when Brown climbed Elder Crack (E3 5c) at Curbar Edge. He followed it up with the Dangler (E2 5c) on Stanage a year later. In 1955 Whillans was responsible for an unprecedented level of high-standard pioneering and, added Slanting Slab (E2), Woubits (E2) and Sceptre (Hard Very Severe), all on Clogwyn du'r Arddu, to his list of first ascents. Patey and Cunningham were active in Scotland, though at a disappointingly modest standard. Whillans returned to the Peak District to lead the Big Crack at Froggatt Edge (E2 5b) while Brown raised standards still further with the spectacular Quietus at Stanage (E3 6a).

The use of nylon ropes, combined with running belays in the form of slings and karabiners, was now making a safer more uninhibited style of climbing feasible. Leading standards in general were improving. On balance the use of pitons, though questionable in most cases today, was probably beneficial then in that it must have forestalled a spate of serious accidents.

In 1956 Brown and Whillans returned to Dinas Cromlech to climb The Thing, then graded Hard Extremely Severe. The subsequent edition of the guidebook remarked of it: 'extremely strenuous. A short, vicious climb of high technical difficulty. Difficulty is sustained, retreat beyond the crux uninviting, and the ground below nasty to land on.' Brown and Whillans also

Don Whillans *Chris Bonnington*

worked out a girdle traverse of the crag, taking two lines of weakness across the great walls flanking Cenotaph Corner. John Streetly visited Britain from his home in Trinidad at about this time. Whillans took him on a guided tour of all the new climbs in North Wales and was astonished when Streetly raced up everything he showed him. Streetly explained that he wanted to sample all the delights of the existing hard routes before he grew too old to climb them comfortably. How Streetly has developed rock climbing in Trinidad is not generally known, but obviously his absence has deprived Britain of an unusually gifted climber. Whillans later remarked that Streetly was an equally good climber as Joe Brown; a rare compliment.

The White Slab incident occurred at about this time, which highlighted the growing competitiveness between climbers. The main characters in this drama were Whillans and Ron Moseley. The White Slab on Clogwyn du'r Arddu was somewhat of a 'last great problem'. Both Brown and Moseley had attempted it from time to time but, in Whillans's opinion, rather half-heartedly. Eventually, one weekend, Brown asked Whillans what his plans were, saying that he, Moseley and some others were going to the Lake District. Whillans replied that he might give the White Slab a try. Whillans had never shown much interest in the climb but was so tired of hearing of Brown's and Moseley's attempts that he thought he'd do the job properly. Moseley had been listening to Whillans's conversation with Brown, and did not tell Whillans that he was still interested in making the first ascent: it was assumed that Whillans, having expressed an interest after Brown's and Moseley's lack of success would be given the first opportunity to climb it. Whillans travelled to Wales on Saturday evening, intending to attempt the route with Don Roscoe the following day. However, he was woken on Sunday morning by a grinning Moseley with the news that he had climbed the White Slab.

1956 was a good year for climbing in the Lakes, mainly because of the arrival of J. Allan Austin who was to become a major driving-force behind the 'free climbing revolution' of the 1960s and 1970s. He was not yet putting up his classic routes, however, and the best new line climbed that year in the Lakes was Paul Ross's Post Mortem (E2 5c) in Borrowdale which was a problem that had previously defeated Whillans. Scotland suffered its second national calamity in two years: Whillans returned to the Carn Dearg Buttress on Ben Nevis and climbed Centurion (Hard Very Severe) having previously accounted for Sassenach, also Hard Very Severe, with Brown in 1954. Both are big, bold climbs on an imposing piece of rock and Centurion has sometimes been described as 'the best rock climb in Britain'. In Derbyshire Brown accounted for the very strenuous The Rasp (E2 5b) on Higgar Tor.

A number of exercises in artificial climbing were carried out in Yorkshire in 1957. These were: the Cave Route at Gordale Scar, the epic on the Main Overhang at Kilnsey Crag and also at Kilnsey, the Direttissima, completed with the aid of bolts. The year followed a similar pattern to the previous one, but with less significant development. In the Lake District Moseley climbed Phoenix on Scafell (E2 5b), and Brown added Eliminot (E2 5b) on White Ghyll, both among the hardest in Cumbria at the time.

Pierre Allain had developed his specialised rock boots, PAs, for use on the sandstone crags of Fontainebleau near Paris in the 1940s, and since then climbers in Britain had used them to overcome some of the problems encountered on the sandstone of the Weald of Kent. But it was not until 1957, when sandstone devotee Phil Gordon started to climb extensively in North Wales, that their merits began to be appreciated in other areas. Joe Brown was so impressed by Gordon's free ascent of the first pitch of Surplomb wearing PAs that he began to use them himself, and from then on their future as the most suitable footwear for serious climbing was never in doubt. They came into widespread use in the years that followed. It should be remembered that the vibram-soled boot was still a comparatively recent innovation and when Brown had first started climbing he had worn the same type of tricouni-nailed boots that had been in use since the 1880s.

Whillans climbed the route of 1958. This was the strenuous and awkward Goliath at Burbage Edge, now graded at E4 6a. It was Britain's first E4 and deserves to be attempted at least once by any climber who has the chance. Together with Hugh Banner's Insanity (E3 5c) at Curbar, it marked the year out as one of the most important in the evolution of climbing on gritstone. Brown added Shrike (E2 5c) to the East Gully Wall at Clogwyn du'r Arddu. Set in magnificent surroundings, it was led in very bold style with one runner in the last 100 feet only. In 1959 Whillans led another gritstone classic, Sentinel Crack (E2 5c) at Chatsworth Edge while Peter Biven and Trevor Peck climbed the Central Wall at Malham Cove using a wide range of artificial climbing techniques, thus demonstrating that virtually any piece of rock could now be scaled given the right equipment.

Scotland's national pride was restored somewhat by Robin Smith's and Dougal Haston's The Bat (E1) on Carn Dearg Buttress. Smith, perhaps the finest climber to emerge in Scotland since Cunningham, pioneered a number of hard climbs there and in the Lake District but did not live to claim the full span of years as an activist he would doubtless otherwise have enjoyed. Another notable Scottish route made at this time was Carnivore on the Buachaille Etive Mor, worked out by Whillans and Cunningham but first climbed by Cunningham and Noon at E1 5b, then modified by Whillans with a direct finish at E2 5c.

Throughout the 1960s, more and more people took up rock climbing and this prompted the development of a wide range of specialised equipment. Climbers in the United States were fortunate to have access to gear of this kind relatively early, due to the ground-breaking work of Yvon Chouinard in the late 1950s. Items were occasionally exported but Britain had to wait until the 1964-67 period before specialised chockstones and karabiners of a safe and reliable design were manufactured at home and readily available. It is doubtful whether the new emphasis on free climbing or the phenomenal rise in climbing standards would have occurred had these technological innovations not been made. To review the history of climbing prior to the development of modern safeguards is to be amazed by how much was accomplished, time and again, in conditions where mistakes almost inevitably led to serious consequences.

In 1960 Joe Brown established the remarkable Vector (E2 5c) at Tremadoc. This is a route up a formidable overhanging buttress on which a series of steep slabs is linked together. These rise in steps around the central, leaning mass. The route threads its way from one to the other, eventually finishing with an ascending traverse line. Thus it tackles and yet avoids the array of roofs it encounters, giving a climb of tremendous character and interest. Joe Brown's eye for a marvellous line resulted in a masterpiece among rock climbs and the name is very apt. This type of climb, the bold, large-scale expedition up the most inhospitable looking areas of rock to be found, was also being pioneered in the Lake District and was a new departure in Britain. The smaller gritstone edges offered no scope for such epic route finding, but there were plenty of difficult problems awaiting attention. One of the most formidable of these was Almscliff's Wall of Horrors (E3 5c). Arthur Dolphin had inspected this on a top rope years before but left it untouched for a more able climber and a time when such problems could be approached with more experience and confidence. A ferocious and poorly-protected lead, the man who eventually tackled it was J. Allan Austin in 1961, who also inspected it by top rope beforehand.

One of the reasons why Dolphin had not tried to lead the climb after making a top roped ascent was that he felt that when it was led, it should be led on sight. Thus, Austin could be criticised for his prior inspection but many innovatory ascents of the past were made after thorough inspections. Prime examples are Kern Knotts Crack in 1897, Black Wall in 1920, and Suicide Wall in 1945. Even today such practices are sneered at and regarded as cowardly in the face of a challenge, a poor compromise between the pioneering spirit and a highly-developed feeling for self-preservation. This may well be so but it is a compromise with a very long tradition, and we are left with a rich legacy of fine climbs while the names and controversies have been forgotten. The quality of a good climb cannot be harmed by any first ascensionist, and it should be a pioneer's right to do whatever he likes, short of damaging the rock, when making a first ascent attempt – be it top roping, yo-yoing, preplacing runners or whatever. He will know if he is 'cheating' and there can be no greater penalty than a lack of satisfaction and loss of personal achievement. Naturally, anyone who completes the climb in good style should be admired, whether or not it is a first ascent, and after all the most important ascent is not necessarily the first but the best. The ultimate 'best ascent' is, of course, the on-sight solo.

Rivalries are commonplace in climbing history, but were particularly in evidence during the 1960s. A typical incident occurred in 1962 in the Lake District. The Esk Buttress on the Scafell Massif towers above a beautiful, uninhabited valley in perhaps the finest location in England. Its main feature is a 400-feet high central pillar which, despite many previous efforts, had deflected all attempts at a climb, forcing them to deviate left and right. Two teams were competing at the time to establish a route that would climb the central pillar itself. One team consisted of Snowdonia activist Peter Crew, supported on this occasion by Mike Owen, and the other of J. Allan Austin, accompanied by Jack Soper and Eric Metcalfe. Each knew of the other's ambition to do the climb, and on Sunday, 17 June, Austin, Soper and Metcalfe started early in order to reach the crag before Crew. But Crew had set out at dawn, and was already established on the climb when the Lakeland team arrived. Crew's route (Central Pillar, E2 5b) was one of the classics of the decade, overshadowed only much later when climbs such as The Cumbrian, a truly direct assault on the pillar, were established. Austin's team consoled themselves with two excellent but less finely-positioned routes, The Red Edge and the tellingly-named Black Sunday.

1963 marked a move towards greater diversity in rock climbing in North Wales. Traditionally, climbing there had meant crag climbing or the frequenting of the lower-lying cliffs scattered around the slopes of the Ogwen Valley, the Llanberis Pass, or more recently-developed areas such as the Moelwyns. But the tireless urge for exploration, coupled with a taste for climbing areas blessed with better weather than the old climbers' haunts lead a number of people far afield in search of promising new crags. The Tremadoc cliffs were already quite well developed and were proving popular. One exploratory trip took Baz Ingle and Martin Boysen to Holyhead Island, Anglesey, where they were amazed and delighted to discover the impressive series of sea cliffs comprising Craig Gogarth. Realising that they had come across a major find, they kept it secret, especially from 'The Baron' – Joe Brown – in order to be able to enjoy the pick of the new routes at leisure. They made a number of imposing new climbs but the full potential of the cliffs was not to be realised until after the news had gradually spread far and wide. This took a few years partly because climbers were not yet used to the idea of sea cliff climbing, and were reluctant to brave the possible dangers.

In the Peak District in 1966, Jack Street pioneered Boat Pusher's Wall (E3 5c) at Stoney Middleton, a bold lead of great technical difficulty for the time. Meanwhile, others had joined the group exploring at Craig Gogarth. Brown had been let in on the secret, and the first phase of development was proceeding at full-throttle. Peter Crew particularly enjoyed exploring the new cliff and he produced classic after classic. Central Park, Red Wall, Big Groove, Wen, and Mousetrap are all famous climbs from this period and the work of Brown or Crew who sometimes climbed together. The new route bonanza at Gogarth rather overshadowed a significant climb in the Llanberis pass called Crucifix, made by Lew Brown on Dinas Cromlech. It was given the grade of Hard Extremely Severe, an unprecedented step, and was undoubtedly very hard indeed. The present rating is E3 5c and it had defeated many powerful climbers before Brown found himself equal to the task. His effort was especially creditworthy when considering that the odd point of aid was not unusual then and he led the route entirely free.

Also in Wales in 1966, Denny Moorhouse began manufacturing his range of climbing equipment, in partnership with Shirley Smith. Being more of a climber than an engineer, he set to work to learn the necessary skills, and by 1967 he was making aluminium alloy karabiners and hexagonal nuts, some threaded on to wire which was then swaged to form a strong, continuous loop. Many condemned this innovation because they felt that it encouraged cheating as it was now possible to preplace such runners from below, thus turning leading into a kind of top roped ascent, with protection too often being guaranteed just above the leader's head. Nevertheless, they soon became popular. Moorhouse's other items included a range of chrome-molybdenum pitons of exceptional quality. In 1967 a considerable number of new routes on Gogarth were devised, principally by Joe Brown, but also by the Holliwell brothers. The latter were newcomers to the cliffs but not to Snowdonia, and their main stamping ground was the Carneddau and Llech Ddu in particular; they added the excellent Park Lane on Gogarth among others.

Ed Ward-Drummond's Strand was the scene of a minor epic, with Drummond completing this hard, sustained climb in twilight. Not surprisingly as the holds became harder to see, his second could not follow. In the Lake District, progress continued at a fairly even pace, and the other big event of the year was a television documentary filmed at the Old Man of Hoy, with a famous cast of climbers including: Brown, Ian MacNaught-Davis, Dougal Haston, Crew,

Tom Patey and Rusty Baillie. It did much to help publicise the sport of rock climbing in Britain.

There was a renewal of interest in free climbing in 1968. The availability of new, safer equipment made it a logical and desirable step, and from then on the concept of good climbing style underwent review with increasing emphasis on rock climbs uncluttered by points of direct aid. Whereas at the beginning of the 1960s it had been considered acceptable to use pitons and slings to overcome particularly hard sections, the new thinking stressed the importance of leaving a route uncompleted and unclaimed if it proved beyond a climber's ability unaided.

The chief advocate of the new approach was Tom Proctor. Stoney Middleton in Derbyshire had been the scene of heavily or even entirely aided ascents for many years and Proctor initiated a drive towards free climbing these and other routes which still continues today. His many achievements that year included Dies Irae (E2 5b), Scoop Wall (E2 5b) and, unquestionably the most famous, Our Father (E3 6a). These climbs on Windy Buttress, involved strenuous and exposed climbing and came to be regarded as test cases for Britain's most able climbers, particularly Our Father, which demands the ability to combine strength and balance moves in a complex and difficult sequence.

An equally difficult climb was put up in the Lake District in 1969 by Richard MacHardy. This was The Vikings on the Napes cliffs, Great Gable, the scene of so many historic ascents. The climb was the first E3 in Cumbria and follows an awkward-sized crack in a face which overhangs at approximately 20 degrees. MacHardy climbed the route free, in impeccable style, earning the profound respect of his contemporaries. Also in 1969, Pat Littlejohn began his now long list of important new routes with The Pinch (E3 5c) at Berry Head and Neophron (E3 5c) at Babbacombe. For Littlejohn, this was only the tip of the iceberg – an appropriate metaphor because his climbs often require not only high technical ability but also an unusual degree of coolness.

In the Peak District, the trend towards free climbing continued, following Proctor's example, with many old aid routes transformed into highly-demanding exercises for the hands and feet, while Jack Street's Adjudicator Wall (E3 6a) in Dovedale became the new test of competence. In 1970 MacHardy visited Clogwyn du'r Arddu, and freed November of its remaining aid point to turn it into a superb free climb at E3 5c, an appropriate development on this grandest of climbers' cliffs.

In 1970 Proctor turned his attention to the gritstone crags to produce Green Death (E4 5c) at Millstone Edge, a very serious route. The name is apt. Yorkshire was attacked by an enthusiastic group from Leeds University led by the talented Allan Manson and John Syrett. They had the advantage of one of the best indoor climbing walls yet built, which enabled them to train and to keep fit out-of-season and during bad weather. 'The Wall' permitted them to raise their standards dramatically, perhaps rather artificially, as brilliant climbers emerged who had never set foot on a crag in their lives. However, the advantages speak for themselves. Between them, Manson and Syrett accounted for most of the new climbs made on Yorkshire gritstone in the early 1970s.

In 1971 a fierce argument developed over an unknown young climber's claim to the first free ascent of the Face Route at Gordale Scar – a familiar response whenever a breakthrough is made by anyone not already established. The general consensus was that the route – now rated at E3 6a – could not have been climbed unaided except perhaps by one of the foremost climbers of the time, and then only in a rare moment of inspiration. But the free ascent had indeed been made; the man responsible was Peter Livesey, making the first of his many invaluable contributions to the development of high-grade climbing.

At Chee Tor in the Peak District, Proctor led Queer Street (E3 6a), a line characteristic of the new, hard limestone routes: steep, fingery climbing in exposed situations, involving a series of interesting and superbly enjoyable moves for the competent. Syrett made the second ascent of Austin's Wall Of Horrors at Almscliff, dispensing with prior inspection on a top rope – the first climber to do so. At Helsby in Cheshire, Colin Kirkus's former training ground, Alan Rouse soloed The Beatnik (6a) which followed on from his solo exploits in Wales the previous year where he had made light work of Suicide Wall and The Boldest (E2). MacHardy had made a lone ascent of Woubits (E2) on sight but was less fortunate when he tackled Millsom's Minnion at Stanage Edge and fell and broke his leg.

Ray Evans climbed Curving Arête (E3) on Clogwyn du'r Arddu, a bold lead up the intimidating rib to the right of Kirkus's classic Curving Crack; but he annoyed many climbers when he named another line Jelly Roll. Traditionally, climbs on Clogwyn du'r Arddu had been given majestic names, often reflecting its Welshness and imposing character. Like so many other climbers, Evans quite enjoyed upsetting the establishment – in this case the Climbers' Club and the mountaineering press – and the outcry it caused helped prove their point that British rock climbing needs its rebels.

In 1972 the American climber Steve Wunsch visited Snowdonia and went home having achieved what is thought to be the first free ascent of Left Wall on Dinas Cromlech. Climbed in the original style, pebbles were used as chockstones making an ingenious form of direct aid possible. However, the route became a 120 feet single-pitch wonder – or nightmare for the unfit – which at E2 5c and hard for the grade makes it perhaps the finest climb of its standard in the country, the crux being reserved for the last few moves. In Yorkshire, Livesey free climbed Diedre (E2 5b) at Kilnsey Crag to give one of the best easy-grade routes on limestone; further south, he performed a similar feat on the much more difficult Flaky Wall (E4 5c) on High Tor. This major development was not matched elsewhere and 1973 was an uneventful year, most notable for Littlejohn's Pagan (E4 5c) at Craig Gogarth, a strenuous climb not over endowed with protection. There was a big leap forwards in 1974, the important routes being the work of Livesey and MacHardy. MacHardy devised Edge Lane (E5 5c) at Millstone Edge, the grade indicative of the climb's seriousness. Proctor had been top roping the line, obviously intending to solo and claim it in due course. MacHardy, however, beat him to it.

Livesey's achievements were staggering. In Snowdonia, he established a meandering and intricate line up the right wall of Cenotaph Corner on Dinas Cromlech. Named Right Wall (E5 6a), the technical difficulties are not unreasonable but the climbing is sustained and fairly serious with long distances between reliable runner placements. It was an extraordinary route, but was surpassed by Livesey's work in the Lake District. His list of new climbs included: Bitter Oasis (E3), Eastern Hammer (E3), Dry Gasp (E4), Nagasaki Grooves (E4), and the incredible Footless Crow (E5) on Goat Crag in Borrowdale. All were bold ventures of high technical achievement but Footless Crow combined all the problems found on the others. It remained unrepeated for some time, and these routes served as potent examples of what had become possible, encouraging others to develop the ability which one day would make such climbing standards quite routine. Due to its famous position, Right Wall was the initial focus of attention but Footless Crow is undoubtedly the more impressive achievement.

In the Peak District, two young climbers who were to play leading parts in the development of gritstone climbing, John Allen and Jonny Woodward, made the first of their impressive new routes: Allen climbed Synopsis (E2 5c) at Froggatt Edge; Woodward put up Ascent of Man (E3 6a) at the Roches. Pat Littlejohn added a whole collection of E3s on Lundy Island: The Promised Land, Blue Jaunt, Stalingrad, and Wild Country. His confidence and ability and his

Pete Livesey's first ascent of Cream E4 6a in 1976; he is
on the final pitch in the middle of the Vector Headwall
Al Evans

authoritativeness in the south west were demonstrated by his Earth Rim Roamer (E4 5c) at Dyer's Lookout, climbed late in the year on rock that left much to be desired.

In 1975 there was an explosion in activity, particularly in the Peak District. Many were beginning to use athlete's chalk to prevent their hands slipping. Holds were smaller requiring greater effort and consequently perspiration, especially on the fingertips, had become a real problem for climbers attempting high-grade routes. The drawback was that chalk was highly visible on the crags and unsightly to some. A few even went so far as to report 'chalkless ascents' but, in fact, it was not because of environmental considerations but more an attack on climbers such as Livesey. Not using chalk became a convenient excuse for less able climbers to explain their inferior performance. Livesey continued to pioneer difficult new climbs: Fingerlicker (E4 6a) at Tremadoc, The Great Arête (E4 6a) on Llech Ddu in the Carneddau, and Tumble (E4 6a) on Dow Crag. Great Wall on Clogwyn du'r Arddu, an old aid-route, was climbed free by the 16-year-old John Allen at E3 6a and is one of the most impressive-looking rock climbs in Britain.

Standards rose dramatically in the Peak District. Allen with Steve Bancroft, produced a long list of very hard routes on gritstone which became the Peak District's classic climbs of the 1970s. Profit of Doom (E5 6a) at Curbar Edge is an overhanging groove, well protected, but with very awkward and unobvious crux moves. Allen established Hairless Heart at Froggatt Edge, a slab climb that was not exceptionally difficult so much as dangerous, unprotectable and almost suicidal with its crux moves at the top. Slab climbing at Froggatt became very popular over the years; the climbing there encourages a certain approach which tends to lure

Rob Matheson, John Eastham, Ed Cleasby at the top of Cyrn Las in the Llanberis Pass, taken immediately after the first ascent of Lubyanka E3 5c, with the camera on self-timer, in 1976

the climber onwards and upwards even when purchase on the rock is almost lost. Hairless Heart is graded E5 5c, reflecting its tempting nature which leads you to some hard, finishing moves in a precarious position with little opportunity to reverse the climb should it prove necessary or prudent.

At Millstone Edge, Allen added a climb of contrasting character, well-protected throughout but relentlessly difficult except for a good resting place halfway up. London Wall (E6 6a) became a new test piece, its reassuring character encouraging even the most timid to try their luck. Few succeeded with the first moves stopping all but the minority and the crux section at the top defeating most. Chris Gore later fell off 5 feet from the top; the climb was not 'flashed' until the late 1970s. In Yorkshire Allan Manson put up High Noon at Caley Crag (6a) which was much acclaimed at the time.

The drought of 1976 was sufficient to dry out all of the routes renowned for seepage while the quarries favoured as sun traps in winter became unbearably warm. A wealth of new routes was recorded in the Lake District by Ed Cleasby, Rob Matheson, John Eastham and Pete Whillance. The last-named made his mark by adding Eclipse (E4 6a) to Pavey Ark in Langdale. The major effort, however, came from Pete Botterill who put up Creation (E4 6a) and Gates of Delirium (E4 6a) on Raven Crag, Thirlmere, a cliff which had already received much attention but never by such able climbers. Gates of Delirium was quickly recognised as a classic.

The dry summer encouraged climbing of all kinds. It was responsible for increasing both the experience and fitness of British climbers and the average leading standard must have risen a full grade during the summer. Allen and Bancroft were at the forefront of developments in the Peak District, and a phenomenal number of new lines were established by various teams. Again Allen climbed two major routes of contrasting character. Nectar (E5 6b) at Stanage Edge was a formidable technical problem, difficult to flash on sight but very well-protected while Caricature (E5 6a) at Hen Cloud was not as hard but required considerable boldness to lead. Steve Bancroft did much the same at Froggatt Edge, establishing Strapadictomy (E5 6a) with a single hard but well-protected crux section, and a serious solo venture up the front arête of the Froggatt Pinnacle. Allen and Bancroft were not only technically brilliant but they were also capable of taking the bold, calculated risks that characterises the exceptional lead and the exceptional route. Of the other worthy additions made that year on the Peak District's gritstone crags, most were the work of Gabriel Regan, Nick Colton, Andy Parkin, and Nick Stokes, all climbers of considerable talent.

The limestone crags of the area had been neglected somewhat, but interest was now rekindled. On average the limestone cliffs were twice the height of the gritstone edges and contained many possibilities for challenging, interesting and hard routes. The valley of the River Wye, meandering through the centre of the Peak District, is full of major crags of varied aspect and formation; you can choose between different kinds of route, whether to climb in the sun or the shade or which look inviting on any particular day. At Chee Tor, Proctor added White Life (E5 6a) and Mortlock's Arête (E4 6a), two more classic routes, while John Allen claimed Apocalypse (E6 6a), a hard climb in a superb position high on the crag. High Tor at Matlock Bath in the Derwent Valley is a cliff of hard limestone with many pocket-type holds on which Yorkshireman Ron Fawcett established Supersonic (E5 6b) in the centre of the shield, then hailed as Britain's first 6c, though later downgraded.

John Allen and Steve Bancroft teamed up to produce Castellan (E6 6b), the crux moves of which involved a leap across an 8-foot roof, after which they still had to tackle a hard and exhausting second pitch. The horror route of 1976, however, was another on gritstone, Mick Fowler's Linden (E6 6b) at Curbar Edge. This bold climb is rarely repeated and Fowler himself remarked that its D.P. (death potential), was extremely high and no one has yet disagreed.

Pete Livesey accompanied by Jill Lawrence, climbed an improbable-looking wall to the left of Deidre at Kilnsey Crag in Yorkshire: the result, Claws (E5 6b) was a particularly fine achievement. At Cheddar Pat Littlejohn added two excellent routes – Caesar and Crown of Creation, both E4 6a, which were recognised as the hardest routes in the Gorge at the time.

The summer of 1977 was not as fine as that of the previous year but there was considerable activity. In Scotland Mick Fowler made the first free ascent of Titan's Wall on Ben Nevis's Carn Dearg Buttress (E4 6a) thus introducing the new standards of high-grade climbing to Scotland. The high crags of the Lake District attracted some attention, and two new climbs were founded on the East Buttress of Scafell. All previous pioneering had concentrated on the flanking wings of the crag, with the exception of Livesey's Lost Horizons (E4 6b) climbed in 1976, but this changed with Rob Matheson's Shere Khan (E5 6a) on a wall considerably steeper than casual inspection would suggest and Ed Cleasby's The Edge of Eriador (E3 5c), along a prominent and imposing arête. The crag had been neglected for some time and these innovations placed it in the mainstream development of Cumbrian climbing.

Deer Bield Buttress is the showpiece of Far Easedale, north of Grasmere, a steep cliff lending itself the practice of Extremely Severe cragsmanship and here Pete Whillance continued the tradition by establishing Desperado (E5 6a). While on the Napes, Great Gable, Whillance added his name to a list of distinguished pioneers dating back to Haskett Smith by creating Supernatural (E4 6a) on the overhanging wall next to MacHardy's The Vikings.

The Peak District was now without John Allen, who had emigrated to New Zealand. Jonny Woodward took his place as chief protagonist and put up: Impact Two (E5 5c) and Track of the Cat (E5 6a) at Bosley Cloud and Piece of Mind (E5 6b) at the Roches. The climbs were very bold and technically highly demanding and had defeated many top roped attempts by able climbers. Furious arguments developed over a climb at Froggatt Edge, where it was alleged that the wire brush used to clean the holds 'must have been fitted with 6 inch nails', implying that holds had been manufactured by chipping. Once again it was Pete Livesey, no stranger to controversy, at the centre of the debate. No confessions were forthcoming but Downhill Racer (E4 6a) proved to be its own justification. Whatever the truth concerning its origin, it is one of the hardest and most popular climbs in the Peak District and a milestone in the development of many reasonably experienced climbers.

Livesey added Mossdale Trip (E5 6a) to Gordale Scar in Yorkshire, while at Bosigran in Cornwall he produced the hard and serious Fool's Lode (E5 6a), a steep climb in an impressive situation. Reviewing his immense contribution to British rock climbing, his versatility becomes apparent. He possessed the ability to pioneer on many different types of cliff and varieties of rock and important new routes attributed to him exist not only on crags all over Britain but also in Europe and the United States.

Littlejohn continued to find new and hard climbs in the south west while Richard 'Nipper' Harrison explored the Avon Gorge. The Focal Buttress on Lundy, situated in a beauty spot at the southern end of the island, was climbed by Littlejohn to give the fierce and very bold Olympia (E5 6a), the hardest climb on the island. At Craig Gogarth, Citadel (E5 6b), an old aid-extravaganza, was freed by Ron Fawcett to establish a strenuous and technically demanding climb, for some time regarded as the hardest route in Wales.

In 1978 the E6 grade was introduced to North Wales. Pete Whillance returned to Clogwyn du'r Arddu to complete a route he had begun the previous year, and established A Midsummer Night's Dream (E6 6b), a particularly bold and hard lead to the left of the Great Wall. Controversy flared up over an incident at Craig Gogarth when Ron Fawcett preplaced two bolts on The Cad (E5 6a). It was felt that they were unnecessary and especially unworthy of a climber of Fawcett's reputation. More noteworthy was Fawcett's effort the following day, when he added Blackleg (E6 6a) to the upper tier, an extremely hard route and very highly regarded.

At Cheddar Gorge Arnis Strapcans and Steve Monks free climbed the West Route E5 6a, a former aid route. The ascent aroused much controversy since the ascent was spread over some six days which many saw as siege tactics. A stance was taken also on a bolt in the middle of a pitch which had already been attempted by Littlejohn as a 150 feet push and had been climbed free to the bolt before giving up. The peg placed above the bolt to protect the next section inspired further condemnation but it was free climbed, though omission of the belay halfway up would detract from its totally free status. Monks, Strapcans and Richard 'Nipper' Harrison added most of the hard routes at Cheddar with a strong emphasis on the reduction of aid to make a former pegging area into superb free country.

On the southern sandstone outcrops, Stevie Haston made some impressive solo ascents particularly at Harrison's Rocks, where he climbed Coronation Crack (6b) and Glendale Crack (6c), the most noteworthy of a number of bold ventures. It is impossible to protect a lead on these outcrops due to the softness of the rock, so top roping is usual and soloing is the less common alternative, particularly rare in the case of climbs of the highest grades. Pete

Pat Littlejohn making the first ascent of Mother Night E3 6a in 1978; here he is on the Space Face at Mother Carey's Kitchen *John Harwood*

Livesey added Das Kapital (E5 6b) to Raven Crag, Thirlmere, yet another magnificent line; and on Deer Bield Crag Pete Whillance put up Take it to the Limit (E6 6b).

In Yorkshire Fawcett came up with two contrasting routes at Ilkley: Milky Way (E5 6b) a strenuous but well-protected crack, and Desperate Dan (E6 6b) an unprotected arête climb from which the consequences of falling are very serious. In the Peak District Gary Gibson pioneered extensively, producing a list of routes distinguished more perhaps by quantity than consistent quality – a fact that was seized on by his critics – but showing himself more willing than most to explore untouched rock. There are many cliffs which offer worthwhile climbing but nothing distinguished enough to be considered a classic climb. Many of Gibson's routes were made in areas of this kind, often badly in need of development, and he should not be criticised because nature took no account of the aesthetic sense of the rock climber. Gibson's critics failed to note one important fact, which was that no one was forcing them to climb his lines. One of his best was the serious and impressive London's Burning (E5 6a) at Willersley.

On the Peak District's gritstone crags Jonny Woodward and Don Barr continued to find significant new climbs, but the most impressive of the year was Paul Bolger's Bat Out Of Hell (E5 6a) on Higgar Tor. The crag boasts some of the roughest rock to be found anywhere, set at a fierce, unfriendly angle with a reputation for ripping a climber's skin to shreds and it is certain to draw blood from anyone unsuspecting enough to attempt it with untaped hands. American Mike Graham put up an impressive performance, making stylish ascents of most of the Peak's modern classics and he surpassed himself and many others by achieving the first entirely free ascent of Bastille (E5 6c) on High Tor. This was Britain's first 6c, and a climb with a reputation for stopping very good leaders.

During the winter Proctor transformed Stoney Middleton from an average cliff to climb aided into a great one unaided, adding: Traffic Jam (E5 6a), Scarab (E5 6b), Circe (E5 6b), Kink (E6 6b), and later Four Minute Tiler (E5 6b), all of which have become essential examinations for aspiring high-grade leaders. All are representative of hard modern climbing on limestone as they are all steep with mainly very small holds, are strenuous to climb and to protect but safe unless mishandled.

There was little climbing of note in the Peak District in 1979, with the exception of Phil Burke's on High Tor, and Jim Moran at Water-cum-Jolly. Pex Hill Quarry, near St Helens in Lancashire was combed for new climbs by Phil Davidson who led a drive to improve standards and soloed Black Magic (E6 6a), a serious route of the boulder problem type.

In Pembrokeshire a campaign to develop the sea cliffs was well under way, headed by Pat Littlejohn. The south coast was the centre of attention, a vast and previously neglected area of limestone cliffs of varying shapes and sizes. The rock is characterised by its unusually good frictional properties and its large number of steep but relatively easy climbs. Littlejohn's, however, were not so easy, and included a series of classics such as: Hyperspace (E4 6a), Tangerine Dream (E4 6a) and Tiger Tiger (E5 6b). In south-east Wales he added Sorcery (E5 6b) to the steep and intimidating cliffs at Ogmore.

Scotland's first E5 was the work of a native, Dave Cuthbertson. Wild Country (E5 6b) is a steep climb with highly technical moves on The Cobbler at Arrochar. Cuthbertson has pioneered extensively all over Scotland and done much to encourage the development of low-lying cliffs which were largely ignored by earlier Scottish climbers because of their preference for mountaineering. In the Lake District Jeff Lamb and Ed Cleasby made the first free ascent of another old aid-extravaganza, Trilogy (E4 6a) which has acquired a reputation as a frightening climb with a record for spectacular falls. Its grade was therefore probably not accurate. Yet another aid climb – and not an easy one – was freed by Ron Fawcett to give Hell's

Ron Fawcett being filmed for television by Sid Perou while making the first ascent of Lord of the Flies, E6 6b, on Dinas Cromlech, Llanberis Pass in 1979 *Paul Williams*

Wall (E6 6c), an extremely difficult new test case taking a fierce overhanging crack on Bowderstone Crag, Borrowdale.

In North Wales, Fawcett established Lord of the Flies (E6 6b) on Dinas Cromlech's Right Wall. Cameraman Sid Perou filmed the ascent with Fawcett exercising remarkable restraint in his use of language, especially when he was having difficulty placing protection. At Craig Gogarth Pete Whillance put up The Long Run (E6 6a) on the stretch of wall left of Fawcett's The Cad. With Fawcett gaining the publicity and acclaim for Lord of the Flies, Livesey determined not to be outdone and set his sights on the Suicide Wall at Idwal. Livesey's style of climbing, though not technically difficult, had always been bold and the Suicide Wall with its virtually non-existent protection offered a suitable challenge. Livesey climbed a line left of the Suicide Wall route, to give Zero (E6 6a). This was certainly Livesey's finest achievement in North Wales and was not repeated until 1983 by Jerry Moffatt.

The limestone cliffs on the Great Ormes at Llandudno had been explored to some extent by Rowland Edwards in the early 1970s. Many of the climbs recorded then had been made using points of aid, and these now began to be eliminated by John Redhead whose most remarkable contribution was Plas Berw (E5 6b) on Castell y Gwynt, a forceful and not overprotected lead.

1980 was an incredible year for climbing in North Wales and standards rose impressively. They also improved considerably in the United States: Jim Collins produced a climb called Genesis in Colorado, graded 5.13 – the highest – but it remained unrepeated for over two years until Briton Jerry Moffatt managed an ascent. Tremadoc was the first area to be tackled and Redhead started the campaign with his Atomic Finger Flake (E4 6b) on the Vector Buttress. Fawcett followed on with Strawberries (E7 6b) attracting a great deal of criticism for the style of his first ascent. The climb follows a thin crackline up the continuously overhanging headwall of the Vector Buttress, and he yo-yoed his way to a high point on the route before giving up for the day. Returning a few days later, he abseiled down the line preplacing all the runners he had used on the previous assault, so as to be able to continue from his high point having expended the smallest possible amount of energy climbing the part of the route he had already established. He managed to complete it without much more effort but laid himself open to charges that such a procedure made the ascent invalid. Nevertheless, no amount of arguing will alter the fact that Fawcett's claim to the first ascent is secure and rightly so. It is a shame that it was not achieved in better style, but Fawcett's most qualified critics are the subsequent ascensionists who have chosen to avoid such tactics rather than to copy him. They prefer to start again from scratch whenever an attempt begun on a previous day has failed as many still prize the personal satisfaction gained by an 'honest' ascent more highly than a success by any means policy which turns a climb into a mere exercise of route ticking.

Redhead soon added Bananas (E5 6c) as a companion piece, a vicious boulder problem 200 feet up. Fawcett turned his attention to Dinas Cromlech creating a string of superb new routes on this magnificent cliff: J.R. (E5 6b), Ivory Madonna (E6 6b), and Hall of Warriors (E6 6b) and Atomic Hot Rod (E7 6b) which were pioneered on the same day. He then moved to Craig Gogarth, establishing The Big Sleep (E6 6b) on the main cliff, again proving his versatile climbing ability.

Redhead, however, surpassed even this when he concentrated his efforts on the North Stack Wall. A line adjacent to Fawcett's controversial The Cad and Whillance's The Long Run had previously been examined and cleaned but it had been left unclimbed by Whillance and others, who knew it was an exceptionally hard and dangerous route. They were not prepared to 'tame' it by resorting to the sort of tactics Fawcett had used on The Cad and preferred instead to leave it for a climber with both the necessary skill and boldness. Redhead abseiled down the line to examine it, realised that it was quite unprotectable as well as being as hard as anything he had tried before but decided to risk making a lead. He gave The Bells, The Bells a grade of E7, explaining that although he was not an E7 leader he was satisfied that anyone who tried to lead the route without any prior knowledge would have to be capable of this standard simply to reach the top alive. It has so far been repeated only as a top roped ascent and remains a tribute to his boldness. Redhead also added The Wrinkled Retainer (E5 6c) to the Milestone Buttress in the Ogwen Valley, an unusually hard and entertaining route on this most traditional climber's cliff.

Pat Littlejohn continued to find magnificent new climbs on the Pembrokeshire sea cliffs including: Pleasure Dome (E3 6a), The Butcher (E3 6a), Barbarella (E4 6a) and Public Enemy (E5 6a). Pete Whillance discovered a climb of unprecedented difficulty for Scotland when he established the serious and superb Edge of Extinction (E6 6b) on the Brack at Arrochar. In the Lake District he concentrated on the impressive slate walls of Hodge Close Quarry near Coniston, slanting at around 70 to 80 degrees and characterised by small, sharp and friable holds. Many consider the place to be a very silly – in other words dangerous – choice for development as a climbing ground but Whillance and his friends disagree. Their efforts have been marked by a praiseworthy regard for ethics in that when dealing with such rocks it is tempting to scatter fixed protection points – pegs and bolts – all over the crag as a 'safety measure'. Whillance's two important innovations here, The Main Event (E5 6a) and Life in the Fast Lane (E5 6a) are typically serious routes, offering beautifully located and highly distinguished climbing.

There were fewer climbs of note in the Peak District but standards continued to rise and two climbers introduced the 6c grade by establishing a number of classic, futuristic desperates: Jonny Woodward put up Plague (E5 6c) at Rivelin Edge and Pulsar (E5 6c) at Higgar Tor; Tim Leach added Moonshine (E6 6c) at Curbar Edge. Ron Fawcett's climbs, though technically not as difficult, were bigger and bolder and he contributed One Step Beyond (E6 6b) and Shape of Things to Come (E6 6b) at Curbar. Pete Livesey demonstrated his staying power by adding The Golden Mile (E5 6a) at Chee Tor, probably the crag's classic, and in Yorkshire Pete Gomersall made a noteworthy new route at Blue Scar. This dangerous crag yielded Death Wish (E6 6b), the name providing a warning for future ascensionists.

1981 was not as important innovatively as 1980 but there was plenty of activity throughout the country and standards remained high. In Lancashire levels were brought into line with those achieved elsewhere due to the efforts of Dave Kenyon at Houghton Quarry and John Hartley at Wilton. An abundance of E5s began to appear on Scottish crags, the work of either Whillance or Cuthbertson. In North Wales, Jerry Moffatt and John Redhead climbed Hitler's Buttock (E5 6b) and Moffatt established Psych'n'Burn (E6 6c).

At Dinas Cromlech, I proved that there was still scope for superb routes by putting up Tess of the D'Urbervilles (E6 6a) on the Left Wall, and John Redhead straightened out Fawcett's variation of Right Wall Right Hand to establish Precious (E6 6c), a magnificent direct line completely independent of the other climbs on Right Wall. Across the valley on Dinas Mot a crackline previously desecrated by piton abuse was freed by Stevie Haston and Leigh McGinley, to give The Red Ring (E5 6b). Haston performed a similar service for Obelisk at Craig Gogarth, free climbing it at E5 6b.

Continued interest in the possibilities of North Wales's limestone crags led to further developments at Craig y Forwyn and the start of an intensive campaign at Craig pen Trwyn at Llandudno. Mel Griffiths and Leigh McGinley free climbed a line of old bolt scars petering out halfway up the cliff and then continued to the top to establish Axle Attack (E5 6a). Due to its

Left: Jonny Woodward on Strawberries E7 6b, and right: Jerry Moffatt on the crux of Void

Jonny Woodward taking one of the four falls off Strawberries before completing this very hard route

nearby café and general suitability for extreme free climbing – it is full of obstacles that seem tailor-made for experts – it is probably the best high-grade climbers' crag in Wales.

Whillance, Pete Botterill, Jeff Lamb and Rick Graham were prolific in the Lake District, adding E4s by the dozen but Yorkshire was the venue for the year's desperates. Ron Fawcett went into overdrive at Gordale Scar. The old aid route, Cave Route, had been free climbed in the early 1970s by Pete Livesey but not without taking rests on runners. Fawcett completed the same climb in a single push and renamed it Tiger Mountain (E7 6b). He added an 'alternative start' – 70 feet of climbing at 6b and 6c – and christened it One Bad Habit (E7 6c).

In the Peak District Fawcett, Jerry Moffatt, and Daniel and Dominic Lee added to the supply of E5s at 6b or 6c standard. Water-Cum-Jolly was the scene of feverish activity on two of its principal cliffs, the Rubicon Wall and the Central Buttress. The former is like an oversized climbing wall while the latter is a big, often loose, and usually serious crag on which to climb. The Rubicon Wall yielded Piranha (E6 6c) to Fawcett and Angler (E5 6c) to Dominic Lee, while the Central Buttress provided the Lee brothers and Fawcett with some hair-raising adventures.

1982 was memorable for the most intensive high level activity yet. Hard climbs of good quality were put up in just about every climbing area in the country, and almost all the activists involved were performing at or within a respectable distance of the most extreme standards. The result of this activity has been a massive proliferation of new routes, many very hard indeed and outstanding in difficulty for a wide variety of reasons. It is fair to say that many of these are impossible to grade for technical and overall severity. This is partly because the first ascensionists come to know them so well in the course of putting them up that they then find it impossible to judge objectively the problems of doing them on sight.

It is very unusual for anyone to pioneer an E6 or E7 without making abseil inspections, cleaning and then trying the climb again and again – attempting hard moves, falling off,

The New Route book for the Peak District, in which first ascensionists record their efforts, is kept at Stoney café. It provides an up-to-date record of activity

climbing up to reconnoitre, coming back down to a resting place and so on. At the end that pioneer knows every move in intimate detail and yet the grade, which is for an on-sight repeat ascent is for a climber approaching the route with no previous knowledge of it. Few climbers are capable of climbing these routes at all, and many are still unrepeated, so there is little likelihood that any reasonable consensus of opinion regarding the relative difficulty of one climb or another will be achieved for some time. The other aspect concerns the different problems found on, say, an E5 on a gritstone outcrop in the Peak District and an E5 on a big crag in the Lakes. Both may be strenuous or dangerous to climb for different reasons yet the assumption is that if you can climb one you can climb the other. This may not be true at all, and the fault lies with the grading system which tends to obscure the variety of problems that may be met on different types of rock.

Jonny Woodward started 1982 well with Beau Geste (E7 7b). This was the second 7b in British rock climbing history – the first was Allan Manson's Adrenalin Rush at Caley in Yorkshire – and involves an outlandishly difficult boulder move using a tiny pebble as a handhold in an exposed position where protection is poor. At Stoney Middleton Jerry Moffatt completed his free ascent of Little Plum (E7 7a), partly worked out the previous year. At Chee Tor Ron Fawcett climbed Tequila Mockingbird (E7 6c) using preplaced bolts for protection: a practice that was copied by others. Raven Tor is the largest and certainly the steepest of the Peak District's limestone crags and offered climbs matching the ideal of the new virtuoso climbers, so Fawcett, Moffatt and the Lee brothers started to explore it. Dominic Lee climbed Obscene Gesture (E6 6c) and Fawcett Indecent Exposure (E6 6c). These were the easy routes: Fawcett established The Prow and Moffatt Rooster Booster both at (or above!) E7 6c, which were a great deal harder: both Fawcett and Moffatt were criticised for abseiling down their respective climbs to take tea breaks and rests after completing each pitch. This is a tricky question of ethics and since most sports allow half-time breaks during matches, why should

Britain chose a strong team to compete against a team of climbers from the United States in September 1982. It was headed by Jerry Moffatt, Jonny Woodward, Dominic Lee, Chris Gore and Andy Pollitt. Here the British team are showing the Americans a thing or two at Tremadoc, North Wales.
Chris Gore leading Void E3 6a *Mark Hutchinson*

climbing by any different? But there are those who still believe that the routes should have been done in one push or not at all. Well, doubtless in the future they will be flashed on sight in impeccable style, but in the meantime they have already been established for the first who decide to try.

Fawcett roamed the Peak District adding E7s and E6s to various crags, while Woodward also contributed a number of E6s. Climbs at E6 and 7a were being pioneered by Martin Atkinson at Malham in Yorkshire, myself and Guy Mclelland on Kent sandstone, Pat Littlejohn in Cornwall, and John Monks, John Hartley, and Phil Davidson in Lancashire. In North Wales John Redhead made variations on Strike (7a) at Craig Gogarth and on Livesey's classic Fingerlicker at Tremadoc (6c). He was at the centre of events at Craig pen Trwyn, and contributed The Bloods (E5 6b) and Burning Sphincter (E5 6c) to the crag, where development was by then well under way.

Plenty of new climbs were being discovered in Pembrokeshire but few at the level being achieved elsewhere. Fawcett, however, rectified this when he paid a ten-day visit and added four extremely hard and very serious routes: Stennis The Menace (E6 6b), Boss Hogg (E7 6c), Yellow Pearl (E6 6c) and Great White (E7 6c).

During the winter a number of able British climbers, most notably Jerry Moffatt and Chris Gore, visited the United States. The main attraction there was Jim Collins's Genesis (5·13) at Eldorado Canyon in Colorado, reputedly the hardest in the country, and then unrepeated. Moffatt succeeded in making the second ascent and Gore was the next Briton to do so. In Britain John Redhead broke his wrist badly while soloing. Jerry Moffatt returned home and promptly soloed Ulysses (E6 6b) at Stanage Edge; a route which has been claimed several times in recent years by climbers who invalidated their ascents by arranging protection in adjacent climbs.

In 1983 bolt protection was widely introduced on the new generation of face climbs on steep limestone. The routes could not be protected by any other means, and it was a sensible solution which copied similar practices long adopted on the limestone cliffs of France, Belgium, and Germany. So far, bolts have been used only sparingly and on climbs where there are no natural opportunities to protect the leader but the innovation upset some, a few of whom even went so far as to remove them. However, the use of bolts is now widespread and widely accepted, and the popularity of the climbs safeguarded in this way ensures that they will continue to be used. In general climbers tend to be less keen on their presence elsewhere – for instance in volcanic rock on the more traditional mountain crags – and many who happily use them when free climbing on limestone would disapprove of their use on climbs with a long tradition of other protection.

In Scotland Dumbarton Rock was layed under siege by Dave Cuthbertson, who finally produced Requiem (E7 7a). The climb is similar to Strawberries at Tremadoc but Dumbarton Rock is twice the height of the headwall of Vector Buttress and overhangs much more sharply. Cuthbertson made his ascent in the same sort of style as Fawcett on Strawberries but whereas Fawcett took a few days, Cuthbertson took weeks. The climbs are also similar in that both follow thin cracklines, and the fact that it would have been unethical to use bolts rather than nuts hampered Cuthbertson further, who dutifully spent much time placing protection as well as climbing. Dumbarton is a volcanic crag, and bolt placements would probably have been deemed unacceptable under any circumstances. The siege tactics were the cause of controversy, as with Fawcett at Tremadoc, but the same comments apply. Cuthbertson led every move on the climb, and is entitled to claim the first ascent. The finished product, in any case, rates as one of Britain's most imposing and magnificent hard routes.

In south east Wales Pat Littlejohn added Painted Bird (E6 6b) to Taff's Well quarry, Giant Killer (E6 6a) to Dinas Rock, and Big Bad Wolf (E6 6b) to Wintour's Leap, climbs which show his ability to keep pace with advances in rock climbing standards. In Lancashire, New Zealander Rowland Foster pioneered some very hard lines, having repeated many Welsh and Peak District ascents during the course of the summer: at Houghton Quarry he contributed Getting Rid of the Albatross (E6 6c).

The most noteworthy activity, however, was concentrated in North Wales. Clogwyn du'r Arddu received much attention due to the fine weather. Jerry Moffatt climbed Pistolero (E6 6b) and then turned his attention to the Great Wall. Here he made a fine effort, linking a set of difficult stretches of rock together to produce a climb as fine as Whillance's Midsummer Night's Dream, but somewhat harder (E7). However, both routes avoid the obvious challenge of the direct line – Whillance's deviates to the left, Moffatt's to the right – which remains unclimbed and which has been attempted seriously by John Redhead only, who has made a number of epic forays up this main part of the wall. When established it will be one of the finest in Britain.

Craig Pen Trwyn was combed for new routes by many of the country's most able climbers. Some proved so severe that the talented spent days in overcoming them while Moffatt took several weeks to produce the hardest of all, Masterclass. Both Fawcett and Moffatt remarked that they had never before achieved such technically difficult first ascents. Elsewhere in North Wales, Andy Pollitt made two very bold new routes: Space Case (E6 6b) at Craig y Forwyn, and Flash Dance (E6 6a) at the quarry, Llanberis.

Back in the Peak District Jerry Moffatt concentrated on the complete ascent of the Great Arête at Millstone Edge, practising the route on a top rope prior to making an attempt at a lead. And Fawcett, spurred on by the challenge of one of gritstone's last great problems, led Master's Edge. In 1984 many of the desperates of 1982 were repeated confirming that the standards of rock climbing in Britain are probably the highest in the world.

■ GEAR ■

The principal aim of any climbing equipment is to safeguard climbers as efficiently as possible. However, it must also be light enough not to hinder movement. Inevitably these requirements conflict, and the best solutions yet found to the problem have involved some degree of compromise. In general climbers refer to equipment as gear.

Specialised climbing gear has a history almost as long as the sport itself. It is fair to say that advances in technical standards have always mirrored improvements either in the use of existing gear or when new and better items of equipment have become available, providing the means to tackle more arduous climbs without incurring greater degrees of risk.

Scarpa Cragratz rock boots. A rigid type of rock boot with a smooth, stiff rubber sole which is slightly domed for friction

Boots

No equipment is needed to start climbing. You can scramble across easy rocks barefoot if you wish. But it soon becomes apparent that the rock cuts your feet and that it is difficult to grip small holds, so the acquisition of suitable footwear must be considered.

While big boots are fine for trekking up and down Everest, a 100-foot rockface in Britain is a different proposition. As low temperatures are not a problem and rain stops play, the ideal type of shoe is light and compact with as good a grip as a racing tyre. Pierre Allain developed the first-ever light rock boot, the PA, in the 1940s. It consisted of a light leather and canvas upper, laced up to the ankle, with a smooth sole made of high-friction rubber. By cramming one's feet mercilessly into them, close contact with the rock was achieved and the rubber offered both protection for the feet and exceptional grip. The laws of physics dictate that when a surface area is increased so the degree of friction is increased also; and like a tyre on a race track, the boot moulded itself to the contours of the rockface. However, the fact that the climber also has to stand on small ledges necessitated a compromise: the rubber was harder than might otherwise have been ideal and shaped quite carefully to provide the necessary and corresponding edge round the rim of the sole, while the boot itself was designed to bend lengthways but not sideways.

The PA did not come into widespread use in this country until the end of the 1950s. Similar boots were quickly devised and the EB came to dominate the market. Virtually identical to the PA, it was easily the best design and sold widely during the 1970s and seemed destined to maintain its position indefinitely. However, the ever-increasing demand prompted the manufacturers to abandon hand-crafted methods in favour of mass production and they also altered the design slightly. The new EB was a noticeably inferior rock boot, and there was outrage in the climbing world when climbers began to slip off the rock where they woud not have done before. Climbers would search high and low for EBs of the original design and rival manufacturers were quick to see a chance of destroying the EB monopoly. By the time the manufacturers of EBs had hit on the solution – to make the boot as before but sell it at a higher price – rival boots had been introduced which were as good or even better.

The new type sometimes performed better than the EB – no small achievement – and also went a long way towards eliminating its only major drawback which was having been designed for the narrower French foot rather than the wider British foot, it was uncomfortable to wear. Perhaps the best of the new designs from this point of view was the boot manufactured by the German company Hanwag, which had a wide, padded upper and was supremely pleasant to wear.

Two noteworthy new makes of boots have been introduced since 1981 and 1982, which both compromise between stiff soles for edging and large surface areas for maximum friction. Whereas the previous two best designs, the PA and EB, were built to perform fairly well in both situations, the Scarpa Cragratz and the Berol Firé are optimised for each. The Scarpa is stiff-soled with strong leather uppers, giving it an unparalleled performance when edging is required; in contrast, the Firé uses very high friction rubber combined with soft uppers, and is best employed on routes where the holds are not very pronounced and overall grip becomes more important. The special properties of each have already been tested on both types of climbs and we are soon likely to hear of the establishment of new routes which will be climbable only in the appropriate sorts of footwear.

To continue the metaphor of racing tyres and rock boots, the racing driver's 'hands' and 'feet' are his front and rear tyres and when the car is travelling at speed on the track the 'hands' and 'feet' react in the same way: the tyres warm-up the rubber becomes tacky, and grip is maintained. However, in climbing the feet encased in rock boots are well prepared but the hands are not. Unlike tyres which grip better when warm, hands react to an increase in temperature by sweating, and the tips of the fingers soon convert every hold they touch into a miniature skid pan. Light magnesium carbonate – chalk – is an excellent drying agent and most climbers today carry a chalkbag in which to dip their hands. Some tend to sweat profusely and consequently spend more time chalking-up than climbing! The only problem with chalk is that it is white and leaves a trail of marks on the rockface which some think is an eyesore. As most valleys usually have a 30-foot wide strip of tarmac running their entire length, climbers need not feel too guilty. At least chalk is washed away by rain.

Climbers sometimes tape their hands to prevent them being cut on sharp holds. Benzoin tincture can also be used to stick the tape to the fingers.

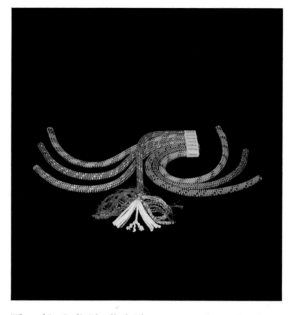

The white individually laid cores wound together form the main strength of the rope. If the yarns are dyed it reduces their strength, and so is unnecessary when used with a multi-coloured mantle. The many different colours make rope identification easier when using double ropes

Ropes

Climbing ropes perform many functions but their chief one is to stop you from hitting the ground in the event of a fall. When falling through mid-air the body soon acquires a great deal of kinetic energy; deceleration must be rapid and efficient. Nylon rope is the most suitable rope and has the necessary characteristics to allow for this.

The raw material used to make a climbing rope is crude oil lying beneath some desert or ocean. The polymerisation processes developed by chemical companies can be used to manufacture nylon yarns with specific qualities. Climbing ropes have to be highly elastic to absorb shock loadings of great intensity. There are many rope manufacturers and each one has its own way of arranging the 'lay' to produce varying strengths and handling characteristics. The rope's inner core is Kern which gives the rope strength and an outer mantle which acts as a projective jacket; its threads are usually woven in a distinctive pattern from which it can be identified when other ropes are used. Colour codes vary enormously.

Climbers today use two ropes rather than one. Double rope technique has many advantages over single rope methods and has become widely accepted by climbers of all levels of expertise. Two belaying systems are far safer than one, and the use of two 9-millimetre ropes ensures that 'hidden' risks are minimised. Much can go wrong with a rope while a pitch is being led: it may not be tied properly, it may be rubbing against a sharp edge or it may have a cut or other flaw but if the leader falls a back-up system will usually ensure that a tragedy is avoided even if a nasty surprise is not. Runners can be shared between different ropes, thus minimising the amount of drag, a serious hazard for any leader. Many lives have been saved – including my own – by using double ropes. Two 150-foot lengths can provide a double abseil rope of this same length, as opposed to half this if a single rope is used: and if something goes wrong which it can do on any standard of climb, the combined length of 300 feet may prove invaluable.

A Wild Country combination of their waist belt and black belt leg loops, a very lightweight harness at 440 grams. With the racking not essential to the harness's safety, climbers who prefer using a bandolier can remove the cord and rings easily

Harnesses

The harness attaches the rope to the body and fulfils three specific requirements:

1. In the event of a fall, the climber ends up in a comfortable and safe sitting position with the load distributed under the thighs and sometimes around the shoulders;
2. It provides a reasonable hanging seat for abseiling and belaying;
3. A suitable means of carrying protection gear.

All three are very important. Equipment must be carried at all times, so it is essential that the harness has loops of cord from which gear can easily be hung. The equipment must be hung on each side of the waist permitting quick identification and retrieval of any item required.

The other two requirements seem similar, but are in fact very different. The chief concern in designing harnesses is comfort in the event of a fall while providing a reasonable seat is also desirable. To prevent discomfort, harness designs incorporate a waist belt, usually about 50 millimetres wide, fastened either with a buckle or a tape knot; and two leg loops, positioned around the tops of the thighs. The advantage of this now standard arrangement is that it prevents pressure ever coming on to the crutch area, even in a violent fall. This universal design permits almost complete interchangeability between different makes of harness – allowing a staggering degree of choice, as there are now over 100 types – and this guarantees that individual climbers can find a configuration exactly suited to their needs.

The most famous type of harness was designed by Don Whillans, and it was the first to be developed with comfort in the event of a fall in mind. However, this is only possible if you 'know' the harness well enough to be able to adopt the correct falling position. High-grade climbers often used it in preference to others but newer simpler designs are now becoming more popular.

Karabiners ('Krabs')

These are climbers' principal means of linking pieces of equipment together. They have changed little in shape or size since their introduction but are now considerably lighter. Early European designs weighed 240 grams and had a breaking strain tolerance of 1800 kilograms; today's best examples weigh only 43 grams yet can tolerate a loading of up to 2000 kilograms. This is possible because they are made of aluminium aircraft alloys which represents a step or two in the right direction – gear which is infinitely strong yet weighs nothing.

The karabiner acts as a link, usually between nylon ropes, or tapes and other items of equipment. Sometimes the karabiner's bar-section profile can act as a cutting edge. Ropes and tubular tapes are more or less immune from this problem, as karabiners of the required lightness and strength can conveniently be made to the right thickness so as not to react in this way; but flat-section tapes are more vulnerable especially when used with thin D-shaped karabiners. Oval-shaped karabiners help to avoid this, but they are inherently less strong.

Although many karabiners are needlessly strong and heavy, they have to be strong because most climbing equipment will break under a strain of 1500 kilograms and in this event the krab should be the last item to fail. The exception, 1-inch thick tube tape, has a tolerance of 2100 to 2200 kilograms, so karabiners designed to withstand 2300 kilograms should be used with it but for most other items of gear – nuts, wires, friends – there is no advantage in using krabs rated at anything more than 2000 kilograms. Krabs fitted with flush rivets must be used for clipping into the eyelet holes of small pitons and bolts.

The strength of a karabiner is reduced by at least two-thirds when its gate is open, and this loss would be much greater if not for its squarish D-shape. This concentrates the load on the stronger side, away from the gate. Karabiners should never be used in such a way as to allow them to open. On the rockface they are unsafe unless left with the gate facing away from the rock with the opening at the top and it is dangerous to use them doubled. An oblique pull from the rope may cause them to rise and twist over one another and if this happens they are very likely to untwist themselves. Short lengths of tape are generally used to separate the krabs, thus avoiding this hazard.

Screwgate karabiners are equipped with threaded sleeves which can be screwed shut to eliminate any risk of their opening. They are essential for abseiling and belaying but bulkier and too awkward to be worth while in other situations. New models have hexagonal-shaped sleeves which are easier to unscrew when they have been over-tightened; and many are wider at the opening gate end which is purely for convenience. Those fitted with quick-locking gates (spring-loaded rather than threaded) are less reliable: to use them to supplement ordinary types is desirable in some circumstances, but they should never be treated as substitutes for screwgate karabiners as sudden, awkward types of loading will open the mechanism.

Karabiners form one of the heaviest parts of a climber's rack. Consequently, very light models are much sought after, especially by high-grade climbers, for whom excess weight of any sort is a major handicap.

There are two types of karabiners – a quick-action snap link (*right*) or a screwgate (*left*). The screwgate is better for main belays, tying on and abseiling, as the gate can sometimes open under strain if it is not locked

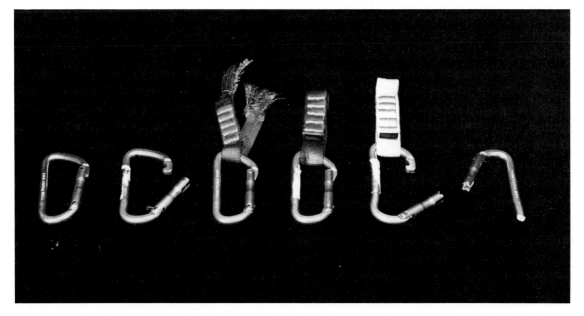

These tests show what happens with an open gate and insufficiently strong tape and how they become deformed under great strain (*from left to right*):

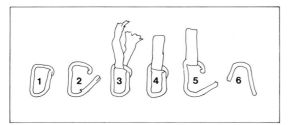

Krab 1. A normal untested Featherweight
Krab 2. Tested in an open gate situation.
     Failing at 560 kg
Krab 3. Tested with a thin tape. Tape failing at 1550 kg
Krab 4. Tested at 1600 kg with thick tape.
     Krab shape deformity
Krab 5. Tested Failing at 2050 kg
Krab 6. Tested Failing at 2100 kg

The Betterbrake in action. The left hand takes in the rope and feels for any slack between leader and second. The right hand holds the rope that has passed through the brake and to the side which will make the brake slide down on to the karabiner and jam if a pull is made on the rope

The Belay Brake

This is an essential safety device. It is used in combination with a karabiner and the rope is passed through and round the U-turn.

The diagram below illustrates how the Betterbrake works. Under normal circumstances (1) the rope can be passed through fairly easily, but in the event of a sudden jerk like a leader fall (2) the curved surface of the Betterbrake allows it to pivot and the rope is cammed and held tight between the brake and the karabiner: the rope should always be held at an angle which supports the camming action so that the Betterbrake's curved outer surface can provide the maximum frictional resistance. If it is then moved back to its normal position the rope will slip through of its own accord due to a reduction in friction. This is the way in which it is used for abseiling, and the outer rim is thick and bulky to allow the heat to dissipate and prevent the rope from melting.

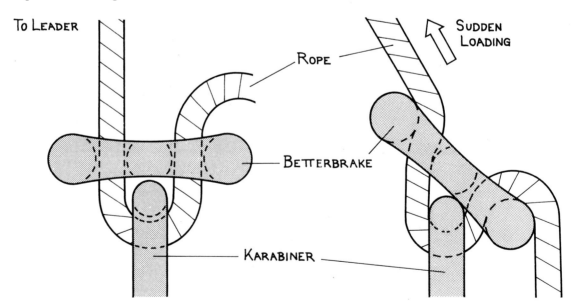

To Leader

Sudden Loading

Rope

Betterbrake

Karabiner

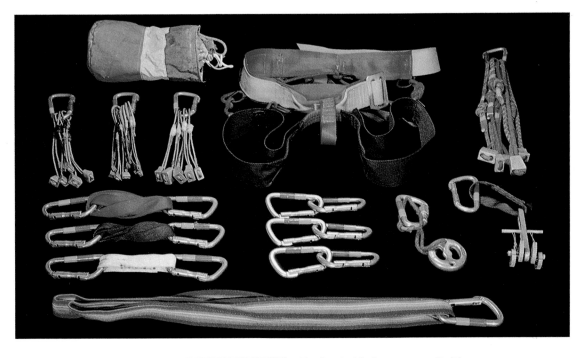

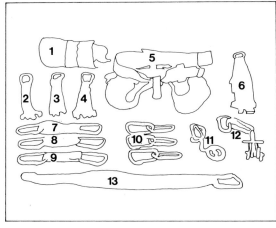

Rack suitable for extreme climbing:
1. Chalkbag
2. Rocks on wire
3. Micro-nuts
4. American straights and rocks
5. Harness
6. Stoppers on rope
7. Triple tie off
8. Double tie off
9. Single tie off
10. Spare karabiners (doubled for carrying)
11. Belay brake (with screwgate karabiner)
12. Friend
13. Long sling

Racking

Some climbers rack their gear on a shoulder bandolier. This is recommendable on sea cliffs as it is a much safer arrangement should you fall into the sea. But a bandolier is a handicap on steep rock as it hangs outwards forcing the climber to exert greater energy while climbing. Gear racked on either side of the waist keeps your centre of gravity closer to the rock and prevents unnecessary strain on the arms.

Rack suitable for extreme climbing

1. Chalkbag: specially designed with fibre pile inside and wire rim to minimise spillage
2. Rocks: five small-size rocks on wire
3. Micros: a selection of RPs, micro straights and rocks
4. Straights: five medium-size straights and American twin-curved rocks on wire
5. Harness: up to the individual
6. Stoppers on rope: five various sizes and types
7. Triple tie off: used tripled up and often useful for extensions on overhangs

8. Double tie off: for extending wires
9. Tie off: for extending wires
10. Spare karabiners: for use on wires and stoppers doubled up for carrying
11. Betterbrake: friction device for belaying and abseiling, screwgate krab
12. Friend: usually small for hard climbs and often replaced by an hexentric on limestone due to the low friction of the rock
13. Double sling: for use at a belay or on a large flake or tree

Nuts

Nuts come in the form of alloy wedges and are jammed into cracks in the rock. In the 1950s some climbers hit on the idea of carrying a pocketful of small pebbles and some light slings. They placed the pebbles in cracks, attached slings to them and then clipped them on to a karabiner. It was not long before these chockstones (often called nuts) were being manufactured as aluminium wedges with a piece drilled out to thread a loop through. Some were threaded on to wire but then it was realised that the wire's stiffness often caused the nut to come out when the rope pushed against the wire loop. Short slings with a karabiner at each end – one for the nut, one for the rope – were adopted but when the nuts were well-placed it was not necessary. Plastic stoppers were also tried but though strong enough they were found to be too light and smooth and tended to come out when not being used.

In the late 1960s, very small nuts swaged directly to wire loops came on to the market. The nuts are of brass and stainless steel ones are now available. In expert hands they can be rigged in combination to safeguard otherwise unprotectable pitches, but are of little use to the less competent because of their easy breaking capacity. The efficiency of stoppers has been vastly improved by the introduction of rocks which overcome a common problem with simple flat wedge-shaped nuts – that placements are often rather insecure – by giving them a concave/convex profile. This simple change means that, wherever placed, they allow a stable, three-point contact to be made with the rock, rather like when a tripod is securely placed on the ground. Because of this they are not susceptible to slipping. The simple hexagon nut has also been the object of attention, and the development of the hexentric a few years ago was a notable case in point: the sides were rearranged asymmetrically to give two different camming angles. They have been somewhat superseded by the now widely adopted friends.

Many climbers carry several nuts on a single karabiner. This means that if one nut does not fit a placement another can quickly be tried. Once wedged firmly, the correct-sized nut can be unclipped from the bunch and attached to a karabiner in the usual way. The rope can then be clipped on. This procedure saves an immense amount of time and energy often wasted by fumbling with separate items on a disorganised rack and is essential in extreme climbing where getting a placement as quickly as possible avoids any unnecessary effort.

Nuts are efficient and can be used in most types of climbing and form the basis of any climber's protection system today. The sizes used depend mainly on the grade of the climb because harder climbs have smaller holds which are fewer and further between, and this of course includes the types of hold, particularly cracks, which are suitable for use as protection points. Thus high-grade climbers usually carry a large selection of small and tiny nuts but few or no large ones, whereas those embarking on easier routes would tend towards the opposite. All kinds of climbers, however, are likely to possess full sets of rocks and 'straight' stoppers, and choose a particular selection suitable for the intended climb.

The friend was invented in 1973 by the American Ray Jardine, a former systems-analyst. It allows extraordinary holding power. Until then all nut placements had had to be inserted in

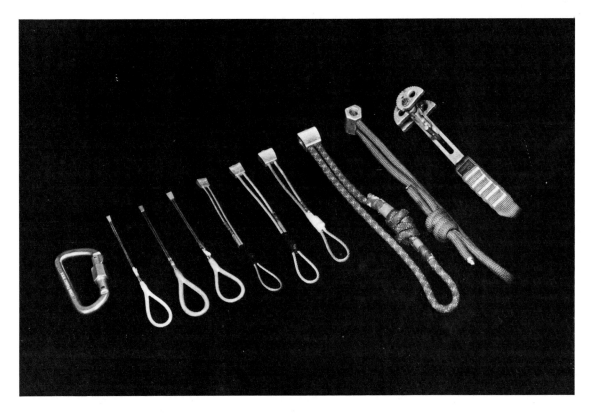

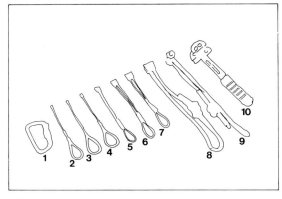

Nuts
From left to right:
1. Karabiner for size comparison.
2. RP 1
3. RP 2
4. RP 3
5. Rock 1
6. Rock 3
7. USA rock
8. USA rock
9. Hexentric
10. Friend 2½

cracks which tapered inwards from above, and it seemed logical that this would always be the case. But the friend converts energy into friction and holds even in cracks which flare outwards and downwards (except on low-friction rock such as limestone, where at least a parallel-sided crack will be required). The friend is made of aluminium alloy 7075-T6 which does not bend easily – important, since many of the components are long and thin – and yet does not break easily even if it bends. The cams have an increasing expansion curve, enabling them to rotate on an axis under spring-loading, which means that they will fit in many different sizes of crack, grip when swivelled and carry on gripping even if the crack expands slightly. A trigger bar attached to the release mechanism allows the device to be operated single-handed. Its only drawback is its weight which is much heavier than a karabiner but this has not deterred climbers and the friend has proved itself remarkably over the years. High-grade climbers will not carry them unless they know they will be needed, but lower-grade climbers who are less concerned with carrying weight may use them all the time. Other similar mechanical devices such as buddies or amigos are less versatile and are therefore used rarely.

Tape

Nylon tapes perform a variety of functions but principally that of slings. These are sewn into loops as this is the only safe kind of join – knotted tapes are not nearly so strong and have a tendency to come undone easily without you noticing. Friends are equipped with ready-sewn tapes but these are weaker than the device itself and are likely to fail before it does when loaded. Short tapes are used to extend runners; longer ones can be threaded through or round suitable natural features found on a climb.

Ancillary Gear

Bolts and pitons are used mainly on limestone and are permanent fixtures at important protection points on some climbs. Pitons have been made virtually redundant by bolts which are cheaper and far safer. Bolts are self-drilling, and competent climbers can install one in little over two minutes. However, they must be placed correctly. Cambridge University investigations show that a bolt must be placed flush at 90 degrees in sound rock for its holding power to be reliable. A bolt head left 2 millimetres clear of the face will render the placement less than half as strong as one properly installed.

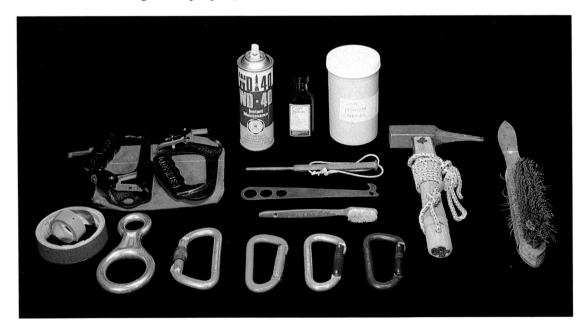

Ancillary equipment:
1. WD 40
2. Friars Balsam (Benzoin tincture)
3. Light Mag. (chalk)
4. Cloggers
5. Guidebook bag
6. Skewer
7. Nut tool
8. Toothbrush
9. Hammer (for bolts and pegs)
10. Wire brush
11. Identification tape
12. Descendeur
13. Screwgate karabiner
14. Coloured karabiners

Ancillary Equipment

1. WD 40 used for lubricating equipment such as karabiner gates and friends mechanisms
2. Friar's Balsam commonly called Benzoin tincture used to help stick the tape to the fingers
3. A plentiful supply of chalk but not a full bag which would spill everywhere
4. Cloggers, enabling a rope to be climbed. Used when cleaning a climb
5. Small ancillary bag for guidebook and particularly useful on sea cliffs when wearing only shorts and T-shirt
6. Skewer for levering off loose flakes, though not to be used with a hammer
7. Nut tool for retrieving jammed nuts
8. Toothbrush for thorough cleaning of small holds
9. Hammer, for placing bolts or pegs and checking the soundness of any *in situ* protection
10. Wire brush for cleaning teeth of 'macho' climbers! Used also to remove moss and lichen from rock, especially on cliffs such as Gogarth which are covered in lichen
11. Plastic tape to identify personal gear, the use of two colours gives a large range of combinations
12. Figure-of-8, a type of descender which gives very good control and can easily be locked to leave both hands free
13. Good supply of screwgate karabiners for inspecting equipment such as cloggers and figures-of-8.
14. Multi-coloured karabiners used occasionally for quick identification of various gear.

Conclusion

With the enormous choice of gear available, developed for a wide variety of uses, the climber's most difficult problem is selecting the most suitable for his needs. Safety is the most important consideration and in the case of ropes, for instance, though very reliably made they are inevitably trodden on, dragged over rough projections, and so on. Though in theory, ropes lighter than 9 millimetres might be strong enough in most cases, you should never push your luck, the word 'most' in climbing can often prove fatal. The strongest items of gear are the tapes, and it is worth the extra expense to mate them with slightly stronger krabs while friends (1500 kilograms), wires (1100 kilograms), RPs (540 kilograms) are best equipped with featherweight and even smaller light krabs.

Climbers can learn by experience only the most appropriate gear to carry on any particular climb but a typical E-grade leader's rack might consist of about 19 light karabiners, 15 nuts, 1 friend, 11 micro-nuts, 3 ties, 1 tape, and a belay brake. The total weight for all this plus harness, boots and clothes would be about 3685 grams. The average lower-grade climber might carry approximately 25 slightly heavier karabiners, 12 medium to large nuts, 4 friends, 4 ties, 4 tapes, a belay brake and a guidebook which together with his reasonably heavy harness, his boots and his clothes would weight about 10,073 grams. The expert knows just how big a problem excess weight can be, and he has the necessary experience to know where to cut corners safely. He will check his wires for fraying, and his karabiners for nicks indicating stress. The expert will also know exactly how to make the most of his rack, especially his micro-nuts which are often used to support a more substantial placement: placed parallel with the main nut on the other rope, they divert some of the shock in a fall and will probably break. In a violent fall, karabiners are often hurled against the rock, the gate is knocked open and the micro-nut will take some of the strain preventing the then seriously-weakened main placement from failing.

Any piece of climbing gear is dangerous if used incorrectly. It is best to seek expert advice if you are in any doubt and, if not, to choose the strongest equipment available. The lightweight, specialist items are for the high-grade climbers who know how to use them and just what the risks are.

CHART WITH COMPARATIVE STRENGTHS AND WEIGHTS

	strength kg	weight grams
Rope 9mm 45m	1750	2402
Rope 8·5mm 45m	1450	2160
Rope 8mm 45m	1310	1410
Harness – Wild Country	2500	440
Harness – Troll	2500	558
Belaybrake	3000	86
Karabiner: Featherweight – open (snap)	550	43
Karabiner: Featherweight – closed (snap)	2000	43
Karabiner: Lightweight – closed (snap)	2300	52
Karabiner: Standard weight – closed (snap)	2500	66
Karabiner: Lightweight (screwgate)	2300	57
Karabiner: Standard weight (screwgate)	2500	71
Karabiner: Strong weight (screwgate)	3000	81
Tie off	1500	19
Tape Sling single	2100	55
Tape Sling double	2100	103
Super Tape Sling single	3300	120
Super Tape Sling double	3300	237
RP 1	360	3
RP 2	540	7
RP 3	540	11
RP 4	810	13
Chouinard 1 wire (straight)	360	7
Chouinard 2 wire (straight)	360	7
Chouinard 3 wire (straight)	800	15
Chouinard 7 wire (rock)	1300	38
Chouinard 8 wire (rock)	1300	44
Chouinard 9 wire (rock)	1100	65
Wild Country 1 wire (rock)	700	15
Wild Country 2 wire (rock)	900	25
Wild Country 3 wire (rock)	1000	26
Wild Country 5 wire (rock)	1100	31
Wild Country 6 rope (rock)	700	40
Wild Country 7 rope (rock)	800	51
Chouinard Hexentric 5 rope	1100	79
Chouinard Hexentric 7 rope	1100	122
Friend 2	1500	115
Friend 3	1500	144
Nut Tool	—	52
Expansion Bolt	2200	—

All weights were taken from little-used gear using identification tape for accuracy. All were measured to the nearest thousandth of a gram and rounded up or down accordingly.

— CLIMBING WALLS —

Climbing wall training is now an integral part of rock climbing in Britain as elsewhere: essential for all who desire to reach the high standards now not uncommon and also important to the social side of climbing. Climbing walls can serve a variety of purposes. Some use them to improve their performance on the crags; others enjoy wall climbing for its own sake and rarely climb elsewhere; and others may combine both in varying degrees. There are various types of walls, some more popular than others.

Climbers are fairly unscrupulous when it comes to finding somewhere to practise. Anything that can be made to serve as a rockface will do. There are two types of practice wall: those that have been purpose-designed and those which could be described as the found object – existing stretches of conveniently-situated masonry such as disused railway cuttings, viaducts and bridges. Such training areas should not be confused with some of the climbing antics traditional among the dangerous sports groups of university undergraduates who scale buildings for fun. In fact, the techniques required to scale buildings can prove to be a hindrance rather than a help when applied to climbing on crags: they're not compatible.

Climbers practise on man-made structures to build up fitness, strength, agility, stamina: they could be seen as the equivalent of dancers' exercise bars.

Of existing walls, the most suitable are often those by a path or roadside. Dry-stone walling, frequently unstable and prone to collapse when disturbed, is left well alone; and more solidly-built walls too well supplied with holds are also unsuitable. For the climbing to be interesting, and good climbing practice, well-pointed walls with a bare minimum of small holds, preferably awkwardly spaced, are the most useful.

The 'classic' among walls adapted especially for construction with modern, high-grade climbing in mind was built at Leeds University in 1964, and cost a mere £80. Its design is simple; bricks were removed and replaced by pieces of natural stone cemented into place. Holds were also chipped into the wall itself and added in various other ways. The Leeds University wall was one of the first serious attempts to build a climbing wall. However, it was still adapted rather than especially built, and though other useful examples have been made in exactly the same way, purpose-built walls have advantages that adapted walls lack.

Enthusiasm for such facilities continued to grow throughout the 1960s and the advantages of wall training began to be appreciated when its devotees started to demonstrate their new-found expertise on the crags and outcrops. However, the problems of adapting existing walls also became evident. Many such walls had by now been constructed and they were often built at the ends of sports halls. People using adjacent ball courts found they were distracted by the climbers. Thus, purpose-built walls were proposed and architects and climbers began to co-operate in order to create facilities satisfactory to all potential users of a sports hall. Consequently, new sports halls were designed with one area given over entirely to climbing, or alternatively, arranging climbing facilities next to 'static' activities such as weight training.

Above left: John Redhead traversing the arches of Bangor College, North Wales. The traverse plus 20 pull-ups on the lip of each arch is excellent exercise for the arms

Left: Gary Latter practising increasingly difficult hand-jamming techniques on a bridge at Newtonmore, Scotland

Below left: Paul Smith on the Hot Walls, Bristol; situated along the side of the road leading to the Gorge, they are of natural stone which has been carefully cemented. Climbers have been quick to recognise their potential

Above: Jules Taylor at Red Lane, Sheffield. This long gritstone wall with plenty of good finger holds provides excellent training for the middle-grade climber

Below: Tony Mitchell trying an extremely difficult traverse on the Leeds University Wall using brick edges for footholds only

Ian Dunn on the Bolton Tech. Wall, Lancashire, typical of walls found at the ends of sports halls. The spectators point out the problem

There are five main different types of walls. Walls made simply of wood, plastic or fibre surfaces are cheap and easy to construct, but do not recreate the problems encountered on rockfaces accurately enough. They are unpopular and cannot seriously be considered as effective aids to climbing performance. Rock walls are made of transplanted pieces of stone and are the most authentic but offer little in the way of variation. They are best used as instructional tools, providing valuable opportunities for beginners to familiarise themselves with natural rock formations. For the expert, however, they are of little interest.

Imitation rockfaces constructed of fibreglass or concrete mould and incorporating inset pieces of natural stone look quite realistic and are a breakthrough in climbing wall development, though bad design can sometimes be found. Large 'rockfaces' can be prefabricated in a workshop, transported section by section, and bolted on to the wall of a sports hall. To install a large set of these is a simple operation, taking no more than a few days.

Right: Paul Ingham on the Dolphin Wall, Darlington, Cleveland, an adapted wall in the goods lift area of a sports hall. Though only some 20 feet wide, the 60-foot-high shaft represents good-quality, long climbing with the added psychological training of real danger if you fall

Below: Jerry Peel on the ceiling circuit at the Richard Dunn Wall, Bradford, Yorkshire. This purpose-built wall has a large ceiling full of holds and jams

The sections, if hinged, can be tilted to replicate slabs, walls, or overhanging sections. The most versatile type of climbing wall yet devised, they can be used for problem moves and stamina training of all kinds.

Plain brick walls offer climbing which, though not varied, is unsurpassed for endurance training as it is strenuous and sustained with the fine edges giving little purchase for the feet. Though 'holds' are chipped out in places, there are many others because the cement is rarely pointed so thoroughly that small toe and finger ledges cannot be found. The uniformity of the wall offers little scope for difficult problem moves, but other advantages outweigh this.

Finally, brick or thermalite walls with inset pieces of natural stone, like that at Leeds University, are the type preferred by the creators of the most adventurously-conceived walls built so far in Britain. They have proved to be the most popular. Many different kinds of rock can be incorporated – granite, gritstone, limestone – and this recreates many of the climbing problems encountered when bouldering; while edging on brick can help develop the accurate footwork and correct muscles for traversing. Although they do not resemble crags in appearance, they have the useful advantage of feeling authentic. They are inexpensive to build and easy to modify if necessary.

Given that serious climbers prefer to train without being encumbered by ropes, floor covering is very important. At the Sobell sports centre, for example, any climber who slips or jumps off lands on a tiled concrete floor. To fall even a short distance is uncomfortable, longer falls are jarringly unpleasant and potentially dangerous. Although not ideal, wooden floors are less painful and the usual kind of crash mat is worse than useless because it gives a false sense of security about the softness of the landing. By far the best shock absorbant surface available is the standard judo mat which has the added advantage of a similar feel to the loose earth often found at the foot of crags.

Use of Walls

Most walls and especially existing ones, are long and low, so they are ideal for practising traversing, and the length of a climb, though never more than a few feet off the ground, is restricted only by the extent of the wall and the stamina of the climber. If the wall is more than 10 feet high, another type of climb – the problem move – can be worked out and practised. This will involve anything from one to four or five difficult moves, starting on the ground and finishing at the top. Usually it requires considerable strength and a highly-developed sense of balance otherwise a harder problem should be sought.

Climbers can also use walls to solve specific problems, for example, someone defeated by the physical demands of a particular move on a climb can practise it on a climbing wall and – usually – manage the climb with comparative ease on returning to the crags. A set of problems found on a large enough climbing wall will provide good practice for a difficult outcrop-sized route.

Training traverses are longer but are treated as exercises and not routes. However, to build strength and endurance and to develop agility, a route will be worked out, preferably of more than 40 feet each way, using two quite distinct sequences of difficult moves, one for each direction. The eventual aim, once familiar with the climb, is to perform it as many times as possible in order to assess your ability by counting how many traverses have been completed before falling off from fatigue. If any rests are needed, it is advisable to take them on the wall, not on the ground. With practice, dangling from overhanging rock with good holds can be restful and indeed essential on harder climbs.

The Altrincham Wall near Manchester is built of thermalite brick, inset with pieces of natural stone and provides plenty of scope for practising very difficult manoeuvres. John Monks and John Hartley demonstrate a standard problem: you place your left foot near your left hand and continue to stand up with assistance from the righthand fingertips only. These problems require suppleness to place the foot on the hold, balance to stand on the foothold and finger, arm and leg strength to ease yourself up as well as plenty of determination

Opposite page: Matt Saunders climbing the Brunel Wall, Uxbridge, Middlesex. This type of wall is made in a workshop and then bolted on to any suitable wall in a sports hall

When a certain number – usually ten to twelve – can be accomplished in comfort, the next stage is to ignore some of the previously-used holds; those avoided are usually the footholds because the arms need all possible endurance training. Stamina traverses are epic sessions for the super-fit; a climber may traverse back and forth 40 times or so, spending more than two hours on the wall, to reproduce the rigours of a full day's climbing.

A climber gauges his mastery of a given move by the degree of control with which he performs it. Control is the ability to move smoothly from hold to hold and any desperate struggles, wild lurches or inability to perform a move in either direction suggest a lack of mastery, in which case the move must be practised until control is achieved. Then it is either abandoned in favour of a new, unsolved problem, or incorporated into a traverse. Carrying large weights while practising has proved ineffective; muscle is built up but stamina remains unimproved. However, small-weighted belts similar to carrying a full rack of gear are often used by many to simulate real climbing conditions.

For every technique mentioned here, there are many more which will be developed by the ingenious and tailored to their own requirements. Climbing walls are nothing if not versatile. They provide a means of keeping fit and developing the dedicated climber's abilities further, regardless of the weather. For those less single-minded, they are an agreeable and absorbing pastime or even just an unusual, interesting and effective form of exercise.

◼TRAINING◼

The best way to approach a training programme for any sport is by first defining its basic requirements. In athletics a track runner has a set distance to cover in the shortest possible time, so training can easily be orientated towards this single task. However, the demands of crag climbing are many. Climbs vary enormously in length, type and degree of difficulty due to the various kinds of rock. To train effectively for climbing you need to develop a wide range of abilities and though this means that a training schedule for climbing will be complicated, and climbing performance sometimes difficult to judge, it also means that the training need never be boring. As well as having to be extremely fit, serious climbers need to develop special forms of fitness suited to their requirements. Combined with technical knowledge and personal experience, this provides the basis for achievement at least at a reasonably expert level.

Leading is the most thorough test of a climber's all-round ability. A typical lead will span 30 minutes or so, and in that time will examine the following capabilities:

As seen below, the basic and equally important requirements for trouble-free leading are fitness and experience and of a certain minimum standard. Experience can be gained by crag climbing in the season, usually at weekends from April to October and on three to five evenings each week during May, June and July. At this time, therefore, climbing itself takes precedence over training. Following a training programme for the remainder of the year will ensure that a climber will be able to enjoy a full season of high-level activity.

There are two forms of training: primary which is concerned with conserving energy and secondary which concentrates on output boosting. Energy saving is achieved by fitness, mobility and balance. Basic fitness covers weight watching, care with diet, the monitoring of fatigue, and a regular sleep pattern. Mobility training increases flexibility so that the climber can use every hold to maximum advantage, find the best possible centre of gravity at all times, and thus achieve a cumulative economy of effort.

Additional balance training is a matter of 'tuning' the body, making it responsive and adaptable in precarious positions. These exercises are aimed at improving style and capability and do not require any increase in strength. They are also an invaluable preparation for the considerable physical demands of secondary training – if this is to be undertaken – which to the average person is bound to come as too much of a shock to the system if there has been no preliminary work. Primary training keeps the body in optimum health, allowing the climber to take maximum advantage of secondary training, knowledge and experience.

Strength is increased by the correct development of groups of muscles. Stamina is improved and monitored by endurance exercises where strength is measured against fatigue. 'Output boosting' implies the improvement of a climber's strength and stamina when climbing. The latter is a vital point to remember as there are forms of strength and stamina training which are useless for climbers, so the exercises a climber might select to improve his performance should always be examined carefully to make sure that they are really suitable.

	LEADING	A typical lead will last approximately 30 minutes and in that time will test the following abilities:	
ABILITY	TESTS	COMMON FAULTS	REMEDIES
Move upwards	strength, mobility	Weak fingers and arms, lack of suppleness	fitness training
Stand on small edges	footwork, mobility	Poor experience, shaking, weak calves, worn-out footwear	fitness training, wealth, experience
Hold on to rockface	stamina	Lack of finger and arm stamina	fitness training
Rest	stamina, mobility	Lack of finger and arm stamina	fitness training, patience
Cope with natural obstacles	experience	Friable rock, inability to cope with loose holds. Damp rock	experience
Protect climb safely	technical knowledge	Wasting time, inexperience. Lack of equipment	experience, wealth
Carry gear and withstand rope drag	strength, stamina	Overall strength and stamina	fitness training
Find easiest line	experience, knowledge	Wasting time, straying off route. Poor guidebooks	experience
Cope mentally	experience	Bottling out. Shaking	experience

TRAINING ELEMENTS

Mobility Suppleness. Flexibility of joints, permitting fluidity of movement

Balance Capacity to balance with little or awkward support

Absolute Strength Capacity to exert force against resistance; bodyweight against gravity via the rockface

Elastic Strength Capacity for power (force X speed). This should not be required except in an emergency

Sustained Strength Often referred to as lactic tolerance; the tolerance to large amounts of lactic acid. Principal effect is on the forearms, and is a common problem on steep rock

Absolute Endurance Capacity for endurance if carrying weight such as gear, ropes. Ability to climb crux moves when already tired

Stamina Capacity to perform dead hangs, to shake out, and to rest whenever necessary

Aerobic Endurance The capacity of the body to breathe in and use oxygen, affecting general endurance

CLIMBING YEAR	
November-December	Pre-training period; maintaining a general level of fitness
January-March	Foundation period; hard training for peak fitness. Training starts early then develops
April	Adjustment period; adjusting from indoor training to climbing outdoors. Critical month to ensure early mental tuning and perhaps the most dangerous month
May-September	Season: training becomes secondary consideration and acts as a substitute in bad weather or if mildly injured
October	Rest month; if the weather is good the season continues; training merely to maintain a basic fitness level

Warming-up is essential for all types of training. Failure to do so has been the cause of most minor climbing injuries in recent years. The body needs time to adjust to strenuous physical activity and tendons, muscles and joints must be eased into a state of readiness, nerve endings must be sensitised, and neuromuscular co-ordination properly established. Mostly, this is a matter of increasing blood circulation. Warming-up routines are similar to those used in the main training schedule and should include a full sequence of mobility exercises, some light circuit training and wall climbing, including dead hangs. They also prepare the climber mentally for serious practice.

Easing-off at the end of a session should also be mentioned. Breathing is always more rapid for at least an hour after any kind of strenuous exercise while the body repays its oxygen debt and removes lactic acid and other waste products from the muscles. Breathing exercises are useful as a means of accelerating this process. Mild jogging, over a distance of a mile or so, is an excellent way of flushing out the unwanted substances very rapidly.

Primary Training

MOBILITY The almost gymnastic nature of high-grade climbing – very wide bridging moves are an obvious example – requires maximum suppleness for fluid movement. Good mobility

Al Phizacklea bouldering at Shepherd's Crag, Borrowdale in the Lake District. Although bouldering can be treated as a climbing activity in its own right, it does play an essential part in any training programme

allows the climber to transfer all possible weight to his feet and use awkwardly-angled holds with ease and efficiency. Even the hardest high-stepping moves are easy for climbers who have developed full mobility, yet quite simple manoeuvres can be very strenuous for those who have not. Flexible ankles can negotiate small edges with either side of the foot and thus increase the number of footholds available.

BALANCE Separate exercises for balance are not very important. Lack of mobility is usually half the problem, and, as with fluidity of movement, good balance tends to develop as a by-product of general mobility training. Jumping and twisting tricks on tightropes and chains can be good fun as well as useful.

FITNESS General fitness is vital. A good diet is essential, based on low calorie intake, everything should be done to avoid extra body weight. First-class climbers limit themselves to 1800 to 2200 calories a day, which is about the minimum to keep them healthy and in good form. Some have tried to reduce this to 1600 calories or less but this was going too far. Their climbing capability suffered and some even developed anorexia. Diet, therefore, should be carefully planned and controlled, and serious climbers should study nutrition. Rest and sleep are also important so that the body has plenty of opportunity to recover from exertion.

Tony Mitchell stretching out on the Leeds University climbing wall

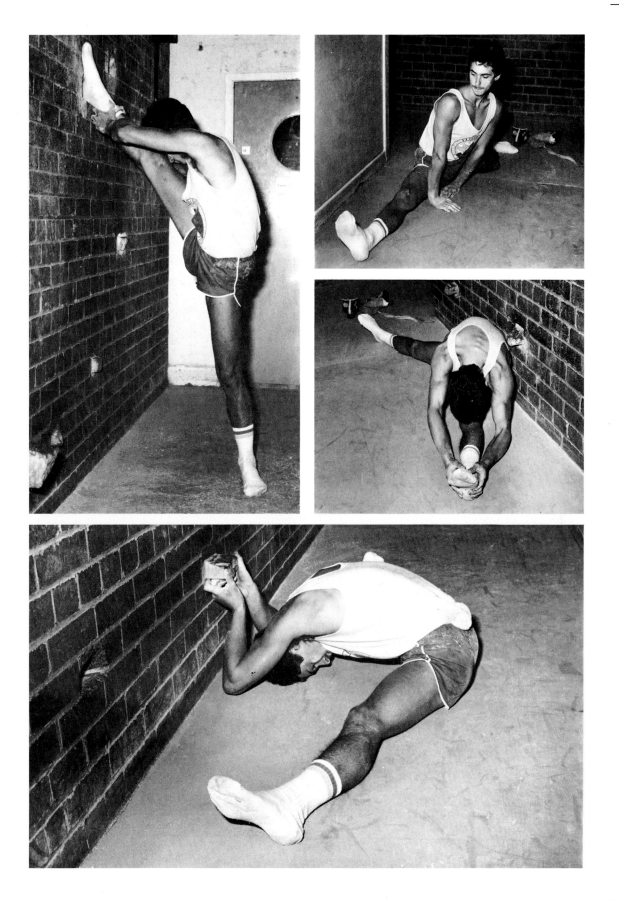

Gary Latter running beneath Cuillin Ridge on the Isle of Skye. The Great Stone Shoot in the background is perhaps the best scree run in Britain

Secondary Training

Secondary training must be structured correctly. If not, it will not only be boring but totally ineffective regardless of the amount of effort. Every type of exercise should be attempted with full attention given to each one in turn, and practice should be regular. This is because each exercise is important to the programme as a whole and if some are ignored the effect of the programme will be much reduced. The programme consists of two equal parts: work in the gymnasium, for building and tuning muscles and work on the wall, the application of the physical development to real climbing problems. Some enjoy out-training everyone else, which is usually of little use. Climbing requires constant self-improvement and as advanced climbing cannot really be taught, it is up to the individual to motivate himself and realise personal limitations.

Exercises

In secondary training, warming-up should never be forgotten or rushed. One result of ignoring this rule can be ripped tendons.

A secondary training schedule seeks to develop the following: absolute strength, which is a basic necessity in climbing and which may be defined as the physical power available to a

WEEKLY TRAINING PROGRAMME			
DAY	**JANUARY**	**APRIL**	**JULY**
Monday	Aerobic running MEDIUM/HARD	Middle distance running LIGHT	Middle distance running pull-ups, dead-hangs (resting generally) LIGHT
Tuesday	Circuits; wrist grips, pinching weights, fingertip press-ups. Fingerboard workout. Fine edge traversing, bouldering on wall HARD	Circuits; finger curls, fingerboard workout, rope ladder, one-arm pull-ups. Wall work: fine edge and stamina traversing, dinks, bridging, rockovers, crossovers, crucifixes, layaways, mantleshelves VERY HARD	Climbing
Wednesday	Rest	Bouldering. Middle distance running MEDIUM	Bouldering and fine edge traversing, pull-ups, dead hangs, rope ladder. Fell running MEDIUM/HARD
Thursday	Aerobic running. Circuits; front levers, finger tensioning, sit-ups, curls, dips, isometrics, one-arm and one-finger pull-ups. Problem traversing and fine edge work HARD	Circuits; figures of 4s, leg pushes, pinch pulls, lock offs, inside and outside edging footwork on wall. Fine edge and gear endurance traversing, dead hangs VERY HARD	Climbing
Friday	Rest	Rest	Rest
Saturday	Aerobic running MEDIUM/HARD	Climbing	Climbing
Sunday	Bouldering EASY	Climbing	Climbing

climber tackling a strenuous problem while fresh; sustained strength which is the capacity to maintain good performance over an extended period; absolute endurance which is the ability to maintain peak performance after a great deal of strenuous effort; stamina or long-term endurance, which is the capacity to remain at or near peak performance regardless of effort, so that exhaustion is hard to induce and then easy to recover from; and finally, aerobic endurance governing resistance of muscles to fatigue, vital in developing overall sustainable performance. These are all aspects of one type of capability but each has its own distinct form of exercise.

Much of the necessary work for absolute strength can be done by bouldering and by practising problem moves on climbing walls. Additional strength is acquired through weight training; building selected groups of muscles by using fairly heavy weights in a routine consisting of a few sequences of five or six lifts a sequence, with brief rests between. All weight training should be carefully controlled as indiscriminate body building can be counter-productive. Lifting huge weights may increase bulk and brute strength but the unusable muscle is as much of an impediment as fat.

The best results will be obtained by those who bear in mind the question: 'is this applicable to a real climbing-situation'? For example, when practising pull-ups, a finger board should be used instead of the conventional bar. When making reach moves, different types of finger grip should be practised even when there are more obvious ways of using a hold. All exercises should be carried out at full reach so that sufficient strength is developed to move upwards even when at full stretch. Thus each pull-up should begin with arms straight and followed through to the point where the chest is level with the board. Equivalent problems should be sought on the boulders and the walls.

Exercises for sustained strength are often ignored and yet are in many ways the most important. The average pair of arms cannot support full body weight for any length of time. A few minutes' pressure on the forearms causes pumping to occur, an oxygen debt accumulates and lactic acid begins to replace the missing oxygen. This causes discomfort and fatigue in all the stressed muscles and at least 20 minutes' rest is needed afterwards. This is not usually appreciated by climbers trying hard sequences on climbs who exhaust themselves by making repeated assaults without resting properly between each one. For sustained strength, climbers should attempt to pump themselves as quickly as possible, rest until they have recovered and then repeat the process. Lactic tolerance is thus increased and improved performance is not difficult to achieve if you are willing to persist. Traverses using handholds and tiny footholds – edges of no more than a few millimetres' depth – are very useful for this purpose, as are those using sloping handholds which are good training for the forearms as well as the fingers.

Once a good sustained strength capability has been established absolute endurance can be studied. Similar exercises are used but combined so as to test the body's ability to perform to its limit even after a concentrated sequence of strength sapping moves.

Thus a traverse using fine edges leading to a difficult boulder problem will produce a similar effect to leading a hard, sustained pitch. For greater authenticity, a weight-belt or a full rack can be worn.

Stamina tends to be built up gradually during the season. A week's training sessions will not be anything like as long as the time spent climbing at a weekend. However, two or three hours on the wall – nothing too hard – will at least help you to become accustomed to the physical demands of being off the ground for an extended period of time.

Aerobic endurance is a measure of the body's ability to take in and use oxygen: the greater the ability, the more muscles will be able to take without becoming pumped. High-speed

John Monks one-arm training on Bolton Technical College wall. A rope is being used to climb up and down on arms only with legs held out horizontally to exercise stomach muscles

Jerry Moffatt doing pull-ups on a fingerboard at Sheffield Polytechnic's gym. Note the hand grip with extended fingertips to increase strength at full reach when climbing

FITNESS TRAINING Emphasis on types and direction of training Minimum bias 0 Maximum bias 10												
	NOV	**DEC**	**JAN**	**FEB**	**MAR**	**APR**	**MAY**	**JUN**	**JUL**	**AUG**	**SEPT**	**OCT**
Mobility	5	5	10	10	10	10	10	10	10	10	10	3
Ordinary running (Distance 2-5 miles)	7	7	10	10	10	8	3	1	1	1	1	4
Circuit work (Fitness)	1	1	5	5	7	7	7	7	7	7	7	0
Weights (Fitness and power)	0	0	10	10	10	10	2	2	2	2	0	0
Dead hangs (Stamina)	0	0	10	10	10	10	10	7	7	7	5	0
Footless traversing (Lactate tolerance)	5	5	10	10	10	10	6	6	6	6	6	0
Footless traversing (gear) (Absolute endurance)	0	0	5	8	10	10	1	1	1	1	1	0
Bouldering (Absolute strength)	5	5	6	7	8	9	10	10	10	10	10	5
Absolute traversing (Without gear)	2	2	8	9	10	10	8	8	8	8	8	0
Stamina traversing (Light and long time)	5	5	6	6	10	10	2	0	0	0	0	0
Balance work	0	0	3	3	2	1	1	1	1	1	1	0
Pull-ups (Absolute strength)	3	3	10	10	10	8	6	5	5	5	5	0
Aerobic running (6 miles fast endurance)	8	10	10	10	10	6	5	0	0	0	0	0
Ladder and rope work (Absolute strength)	3	3	10	10	10	10	8	8	8	8	5	0

running, over distances of four miles or more, is ideal for improving aerobic capacity, eliminating excess weight and giving forearms and fingers a welcome rest.

Skin care: skin, of course, is easily hurt. Although sometimes hard to believe, a cut fingertip, for a high-grade climber in training will necessitate two or three weeks' rest. Imagine 75 kilograms of body-weight accelerating downwards at 9.81 metres a second and an area the size of one or two fingertips rubbing against the rock, then the result – if they are fingertips – is a bad cut. Pulling up on 'sweated' holds is often the cause which is why not using chalk is considered antisocial on many climbing walls and at bouldering areas. Sharp holds are also a problem but, when necessary, climbers protect their fingers with tape. As a general rule, hands should be kept dry for at least two hours before a training session.

Gary Gibson traversing around the Devil's Limekiln on Lundy Island. Pleasant surroundings in which to 'pump out'

Conclusion

There can be no fixed formula for climbing training; every climber is an individual and, in the absence of coaches, climbers must be able to devise their own exercise programmes. They must be able to assess accurately their own strengths and weaknesses, correct their faults and know what they are aiming for at all times. Only then will they be able to concentrate effectively on the relevant exercises and in the right proportions, and so bring about the desired improvements in standards without wasting effort. For the diligent, the reward will be safe and stylish climbing on any type of rock in any part of the country. The less diligent will achieve mixed results, or none at all and those who dislike training will no doubt continue to climb either well or badly. To say that training is essential in order to climb is, of course, ridiculous. Like rock climbing, it should be approached with enthusiasm and if not, a day in the pub is likely to be far more enjoyable.

▬ BOULDERING ▬

Bouldering in Britain can be very varied because of the diversity of rock types found; the size, steepness and texture of the rock dictate a particular style of climbing. Not all rock is suitable for bouldering since the very nature of the sport demands very compact rock. However, there are four main types of rock which come in a variety of forms to give superb bouldering: sandstone, gritstone, limestone and igneous rock.

SANDSTONE: This is traditionally a bouldering type of rock since it is not very strong and is unable to support protection adequately. The softer varieties of sandstone found in Kent, Northumberland, Cheshire and south-east Wales contain plenty of holds. These, however, soon wear away or break off to give climbing on large but rounded holds, usually on very steep rock. The harder sandstone found in the Merseyside area is mainly quarried and therefore vertical and flat with small ripples. This gives rise to face climbing on small holds and is similar to climbing on an indoor brick climbing wall.

GRITSTONE: Geologically this is very similar to sandstone but the bonding of the grains is stronger and it is therefore rougher to the touch. The added coarseness, though, provides superb frictional qualities for both hands and feet. The gritstone edges of Derbyshire and Yorkshire offer very good bouldering problems and particularly test your ability to use friction on flat or rounded holds. The landings are varied to give either amusing or very serious climbing.

LIMESTONE: Although limestone cliffs are often very high and steep, the problems encountered in the first 20 feet make it very suitable for bouldering. The rock offers small, sharp holds which quickly become smooth making good footwork a necessity. Since many limestone cliffs overhang, the lower sections stay dry in the rain and are therefore a good alternative to climbing walls offering plenty of problems and traverses. They also have small caves with endless possibilities for practising moves around the insides of the caves and boulderers are well known for spending years exploring the moves and sequences inside a particular cave.

IGNEOUS ROCK: The mountains of Britain largely consist of many forms of igneous rock such as gabbro on Skye, rhyolite in Wales, the andesitic lavas of the Lakes. The rock is hard, sharp and compact and can be very painful for the fingers. Mountain areas contain many boulderfields where large rockfalls have deposited boulders on the valley floor. Occasionally very large boulders have stayed intact and Bowderstone in the Lakes and the Cromlech Boulders in Wales are famous examples. In many cases the boulders will have rarely been climbed before and are therefore even more interesting.

Other rock types such as slate and quartzite offer good climbing yet have little scope for bouldering but they do present a challenge and are occasionally sampled from time to time by the enthusiastic boulderer.

Guy Mclelland on the Fandango Wall, Bowles Rocks, Kent

Dave Cuthbertson at Dumbarton Boulders, Dumbarton, Scotland

Gary Dunne on the Bluebell Wall, The Breck, Wallasey, Merseyside

Bob Smith on The Sorcerer, Back Bowden Doors, Northumberland

Gary Latter at Coire Lagan, Isle of Skye, Scotland

Rob Gawthorpe on Ken's Arête, Shipley Glen,
Yorkshire

Dominic Lee in Tom's Cave, Stoney Middleton,
Derbyshire

Bill Wayman, Malcolm Campbell and Paul Clark in the Pidgeon's Cave, Great Ormes, North Wales

Tony Penning on Scabs, Penallta,
south-east Wales

Andy Wiggans in the Bowderstone Quarry,
Borrowdale, Lake District

FACHWEN Martin Crook, Llanberis, North Wales

Pine Tree Wall

Shorter's Overhang

Basil's Boulders

Electrocution Wall

1. THE SNOWDON HORSESHOE Snowdonia, North Wales

2. THE ORDINARY ROUTE Billy Bollweavill, Idwal Slabs, Snowdonia, North Wales

3. OVERLAPPING RIB ROUTE Gerry Lynch, Tryfan East Face, Snowdonia, North Wales

4. CIOCH NOSE Andrew Sommerville, Sron na Ciche, Isle of Skye, Scotland

5. AMPHITHEATRE BUTTRESS Dave Whitfield, Craig yr Ysfa, Carneddau, North Wales

6. JANUARY JIGSAW Graeme Thirwell, Buachaille Etive Mor, Glencoe, Scotland

7. TRAFALGAR WALL Julie Gordon, Birchen's Edge, Peak District

8. ROCKER ROUTE Doc O'Brien, Lliwedd, Snowdonia, North Wales

9. THE WASDALE CRACK Penny Melville, Napes Needle, Wasdale, Lake District

10. THE CUILLIN RIDGE John Goslin, Cuillin Hills, Isle of Skye, Scotland

11. OCHRE SLAB Mike Trebble, Bosigran, West Penwith, Cornwall

12. LITTLE CROWBERRY Andy Scrase, Laddow Rocks, Bleaklow, Peak District

13. HERFORD'S ROUTE Andrea Wright, The Pagoda, Kinder Scout, Peak District

14. ARDUS Bob Wightman, Shepherd's Crag, Borrowdale, Lake District

15. THE APPIAN WAY Dave Kirby, Pillar Rock, Ennerdale, Lake District

16. ARCH SLAB John Delamont, Three Cliffs, Gower, South Wales

17. COPOUT Nick Lander, The Pinnacle, Long Quarry Point, Devon

18. ENIGMA Steve Ross, Polldubh Crags, Glen Nevis, Scotland

19. ZELDA Adrian Welsford, Wintour's Leap, Wye Valley, Gloucestershire

20. BLUE SKY Greg Forward, Saddle Head, Pembroke, South Wales

21. LONG LAYBACK Andy Meyers, Harrison's Rocks, Groombridge, Sussex

22. MAGICAL MYSTERY TOUR Matt Saunders, Berry Head, Torbay, Devon

23. OVERHANGING BASTION Iian Williamson, Castle Rock, Thirlmere, Lake District

24. GREAT WESTERN Nigel Birtwell, Almscliff Crag, Lower Wharfedale, Yorkshire

25. TIME AND MOTION MAN Bill Birkett, Armathwaite, Eden Valley, Cumbria

26. CLEOPATRA Christine Murray, Buckstone How, Buttermere, Lake District

27. BOTANY BAY Kelvin Charman, Subluminal Cliff, Swanage, Dorset

28. OCTO Dave Lawson, Clogwyn du'r Arddu, Snowdonia, North Wales

29. PROSTRATION Paul Cornforth, Ramshaw Rocks, Staffordshire

30. FRATRICIDE WALL Lynn Rogers, Carreg Alltrem, Snowdonia, North Wales

31. HARDING'S SUPER DIRECT Andrew Thomas, Stanage Edge, Peak District

32. PROMONTORY NOSE Ian Parsons, Black Rocks, Cromford, Peak District

33. GOING BAD Pete Chadwick, Craig y Forwen, Llangollen, North Wales

34. CHEQUERS BUTTRESS Choe Brooks, Froggatt Edge, Peak District

35. DAWN Gary McCandlish, Wilton One, Bolton, Lancashire

36. THE BOLERO Mick Brothers, Bird Rock, Cader Idris, Wales

37. ROCK DANCER Mark Edwards, Kenidjack Castle, West Penwith, Cornwall

38. LEOPARD'S CRAWL Al Phizacklea, Dow Crag, Coniston, Lake District

39. GIMMER STRING Andy Hyslop, Gimmer Crag, Langdale, Lake District

40. NORTH WEST PASSAGE Keith Robertson, Castell Helen, Gogarth, Anglesey

41. MOJO Ian Fox, Craig y Forwyn, North Wales

42. THE OVERHANGING CRACK Bob Smith, Bowden Doors, Northumberland

43. AMERICAN DREAM Rowland Edwards, Zawn Kellys, West Penwith, Cornwall

44. SATAN'S SLIP Adam Hudson, Devil's Slide, Island of Lundy

45. LORD OF THE RINGS Andy Wiggans, East Buttress, Scafell, Lake District

46. THE TOOL Graeme Allen, Boulder Ruckle, Swanage, Dorset

47. THE DANGLER Rob Knight, Lower Falcon Crag, Borrowdale, Lake District

48. EXTERMINATING ANGEL Lydia Bradey, Sea Walls, Avon Gorge, Bristol

49. DEVOTEE Dave Towse, Gogarth Pinnacle, Gogarth, Anglesey

50. BRAZEN BUTTRESS John Hartley, Mother Carey's Kitchen, Pembroke, South Wales

51. **BRAINBITER** Damion Carroll, The Pinnacle Bay, Cheddar Gorge, Somerset

52. JABBERWOCKY Paul Williams, Craig yr Ogof, Cwm Silyn, Snowdonia

53. CRUMPET CRACK Gaz Healey, Helsby, Cheshire

54. GRANDE PLAGE Steve Lewis, Carn Barra, West Penwith, Cornwall

55. INSANITY Chris Nicholson, Curbar Edge, Peak District

56. SILLY ARÊTE Paul Cropper, Pant Ifan, Tremadoc, North Wales

57. MULATTO WALL Pete Livesey, Malham Cove, Yorkshire

58. CONTROLLED BURNING Gary Gibson, Torrey Canyon, Island of Lundy

59. ARMS RACE Steve Findlay, Unknown Wall, Avon Gorge, Bristol

60. FINGER PRINT Alun Richardson, Ogmore, Glamorgan, South Wales

61. QUIETUS Mark Stokes, Stanage Edge, Peak District

62. PLEASURE DOME Richard Harrison, Stennis Head, Pembroke, South Wales

63. HOLE OF CREATION Andy Newton, Little Ormes, Llandudno, North Wales

64. KINGDOM COME Pete O'Donovan, Stoney Middleton, Peak District

65. HIGH PERFORMANCE Colin Gilchrist, Cave Crag, Dunkeld, Scotland

66. NO RED TAPE Macolm Campbell, Pen Trwyn, Great Ormes, North Wales

67. Dinas Cromlech, Llanberis Pass, North Wales. (*From left to right*): Memory Lane, Ian Saville; Left Wall, Andy Meyers; Resurrection, 'Smiler' Cuthbertson; Cenotaph Corner, Mike Wilkins; Right Wall, Paul Saville; Cemetery Gates, Nigel Preston

68. STROLL ON Ian Jones, Clogwyn y Grochan, Llanberis Pass, Snowdonia

69. THE KNOCK John Allen, Burbage South, Peak District

70. THE AXE Martin Crook, Clogwyn du'r Arddu, Snowdonia, North Wales

71. TOP GEAR George Smith, Threshwaite Cove, High Street, Lake District

72. THE FÜHRER Spider Mackenzie, Creag Dubh, Newtonmore, Scotland

73. SULTANS OF SWING Jules Taylor, Bwlch y Moch, Tremadoc, North Wales

74. PIGS ON THE WING Mark Leach, Wilton Two, Bolton, Lancashire

75. COMES THE DERVISH Kevin Howett, Vivian Quarry, Llanberis, North Wales

76. AXLE ATTACK Matt Boyer, Pen Trwyn, Great Ormes, North Wales

77. BEHEMOTH Steve Lewis, Water cum Jolly, Peak District

78. COVENTRY STREET Daniel Lee, Millstone Edge, Peak District

79. INFIDEL Guy Mclelland, High Rocks, Royal Tunbridge Wells, Kent

80. HUNGER Mark Lynden, Main Cliff, Gogarth, Anglesey

81. MAGIC IN THE AIR Nick Dixon, Highcliff Nab, North York Moors

82. LIFE IN THE FAST LANE Ed Cleasby, Hodge Close, Coniston, Lake District

83. TALES OF YANKEE POWER Phil Burke, High Tor, Matlock Bath, Peak District

84. INCANTATIONS Pete Whillance, Tophet Wall, Great Gable, Lake District

85. GIANT KILLER Pat Littlejohn, Glamorgan, South Wales

86. THE GOLDEN MILE Chris Hamper, Chee Tor, Cheedale, Peak District

87. PARADISE LOST Steve Monks, Sunset Buttress, Cheddar Gorge, Somerset

88. COSMOPOLITAN Gary Latter, Glen Nevis, Lochaber, Scotland

89. **PIRANHA** Quentin Fisher, Rubicon Wall, Peak District

90. TOBACCO ROAD David Jones, Bowles Rocks, Crowborough, Sussex

91. BLACK MAGIC Joe Healey, Pex Hill, Widnes, Merseyside

92. BLOODSTONE Simon Nadin, The Roches, Peak District

93. ROADRUNNER Andy Pollitt, High Tor, Matlock Bath, Peak District

94. INDECENT EXPOSURE Dominic Lee, Raven Tor, Peak District

95. TIGER MOUNTAIN Phil Davidson, Gordale Scar, Yorkshire

96. ADRENALIN RUSH Allan Manson, Caley Crag, Yorkshire

97. THE GREAT WHITE Mick Lovatt, White Tower, Mother Carey's Kitchen, Pembroke, South Wales

98. REQUIEM Dave Cuthbertson, Dumbarton Rock, Dumbarton, Scotland

99. LITTLE PLUM Tim Freeman, Stoney Middleton, Peak District

100. THE BELLS, THE BELLS John Redhead, North Stack Wall, Gogarth, Anglesey

▬ PLATE CAPTIONS ▬

1. The easiest route included in this book, it illustrates the narrow borderline between scrambling and rock climbing. The Snowdon Horseshoe, a splendid expedition taking in the summits of Crib Goch, Snowdon, and Lliwedd leads back to Llyn Llydaw, often at sunset, by way of this admirable viewpoint. Much of the route is a walk but there are some good scrambling sections which are surprisingly steep and exposed

2. Billy Bollweavill climbing the Ordinary Route Difficult on the Idwal Slabs, in typical Snowdonia weather conditions. The slabs quickly become a water chute in the rain and climbing them is a very wet experience no matter how well equipped the climber. Ascents like this are part of the great tradition of British mountaineering

3. The east face of Tryfan offers many interesting and varied lower grade climbs. The general topography allows long pitches which give a greater sense of exposure and make the long routes quicker to climb

4. The Cioch Nose, Very Difficult, was first climbed by H. Harland and Ashley Abraham in 1907. This magnificent route takes the most striking line to the small summit of the Cioch. Andrew Sommerville is standing precariously on the most exposed section of the climb: the nose itself

5. Amphitheatre Buttress, Very Difficult, first climbed in 1905 by the Abraham brothers, is one of Wales's great classics. Dave Whitfield is on the most exposed part of this 1000 feet route, gaining the pinnacle at 700 feet. Although there is much scrambling the rock pitches provide entertaining moves in a grand setting, with the scenic splendour of the amphitheatre below

6. The Rannoch Wall on the Buachaille Etive Mor is one of Scotland's finest large faces. In the summer of 1983 a roadsign found its way three-quarters of the way up this 3500 feet high mountain, providing much amusement. Here Graeme Thirwell is using the post to advantage while starting the short traverse on January Jigsaw, Very Difficult

7. Trafalgar Wall, Very Difficult, is one of the oldest routes on Birchen's Edge, first climbed in the late-1920s. This fine gritstone crag offers a large selection of lower grade, high-quality routes at reasonable angles, some with protection, some without

8. The famous North Wales pioneer, James Merriman Archer Thomson, established a series of classics on this most magnificent of Welsh cliffs, of which Rocker Route (1908) is a fine example. Climbing on Lliwedd is often very entertaining. The sheer size of the routes averaging 1000 feet give them a strong mountaineering flavour, and the usual greasiness of the rock requires a careful, thoughtful approach. All routes finish on the summit ridge with staggering views and spectacular colours at sunset. Here Doc O'Brien is pulling on to the summit ridge after 11 pitches and many hours of climbing

9. The Wasdale Crack Route Hard Very Difficult is one of Britain's most famous rock climbs and was first climbed, solo, by W. P. Haskett Smith in 1886. It has become increasingly difficult over the years mainly due to the rock becoming more and more polished and the grips are now very slippery. It is customary to do a headstand on top of the Needle, but once up there you don't feel quite so brave!

10. The traverse of the main Cuillin Ridge is a formidable task even for the fittest of climbers. Though only of Severe standard overall and not technically demanding, it is six miles long and involves 10,000 feet of ascent. L. C. Shadbolt and A. C. McLaren took 16 hours and 45 minutes to complete it for the first time which is still a very respectable time

11. Mike Trebble climbing Ochre Slab at Bosigran. He is including the introductory pitch up to the starting point which is often missed out and gives entertaining climbing close to the sea. Bosigran is famed both for its easy and hard climbs of character and quality, all on excellent granite

12. Andy Scrase on the crux of Little Crowberry, Severe, at Laddow Rocks, a crag with a very long climbing tradition; it boasts many lower grade gritstone climbs of great character in an isolated valley with splendid views over the northern Peak District

13. Herford's Route, Hard Severe, first climbed by Siegfried Herford, a leading British pioneer in the years leading up to the First World War. The Pagoda is on the summit plateau of Kinder Scout and is one of the larger examples of the peculiar rock formations found there

14. Shepherd's Crag has many classic climbs both easy and extreme. Ardus, Hard Severe, takes a prominent groove to where thin, precarious moves, as illustrated here, bear left to the top

15. Pillar Rock, a traditional mountain crag for climbers, has many climbs ideal for middle and lower

grade levels. Dave Kirby on the Appian Way, Hard Severe, first climbed in 1923 by Harry Kelly who wrote the first guidebook to Pillar in the same year

16. The Three Cliffs Bay typifies the area's attractive juxtaposition of climbs with flat sandy beaches, an unusual feature of sea cliffs in Britain

17. Nick Lander making the first ascent of Copout, Hard Severe, at Long Quarry Point. The pinnacle has suffered a major rockfall which has exposed the brightly-coloured section of rock in the foreground and so provided scope for new routes in this well-developed area

18. Enigma follows a beautiful line on High Crag slabs, which overlooks the rest of the Polldubh Crags scattered across the hillside. A succession of routes on some of these can be linked to provide a long climbing approach to this most formidable and magnificently situated cliff

19. Zelda, Mild VS, is typical of the climbing found at Wintour's Leap; steep sections interspersed with breaks, and pitches which are generally rather sparsely protected. First climbed by J. Grieve in May 1961, the first of his many fine contributions to Wye Valley climbing during the next four years

20. Blue Sky, VS 4b, one of the best Very Severes in Pembroke, takes the rib on the right edge of Saddle Head, which is a large steep cliff with enormous handholds

21. Andy Meyers, south-east superstar, romping up Long Layback 4c, at Harrison's Rocks, in traditional style. Harrison's and other outcrops often necessitate this technique which is much more strenuous on this kind of soft sandstone. The technique must be perfected before harder climbs can be tackled; once conquered the climber can enjoy almost complete freedom of choice concerning what he can realistically expect to be able to climb

22. Matt Saunders energetically engaged on Magical Mystery Tour. This sea cliff traverse can be made regardless of the tide, but the water level considerably affects its overall difficulty: at low tide it is no more than a severe solo, at high tide it requires HVS leading and seconding ability. The traverse is broken in places, but when linked together gives nearly 8000 feet of climbing.

23. Overhanging Bastion VS 4c was first climbed by Jim Birkett in 1939. This classic VS, a superb climb up steep rock and one of the most popular routes in the Lake District

24. Great Western at Almscliff VS 5a, first climbed by Arthur Dolphin in 1943. Forty years later Nigel Birtwell enjoys the delights of this magnificent classic for its grade

25. Bill Birkett, son of the Lakeland Pioneer Jim Birkett, steaming up Time and Motion Man VS 5a. This sandstone face is used extensively in the summer evenings by the Carlisle mob for training and bouldering. The steepness of the crag, the *in situ* sand pit, and the hungry midges make this an idyllic spot

26. Cleopatra HVS 5a on Buckstone How, situated at

the top of Honister Pass overlooking Buttermere. First climbed in 1949 by Bill Peascod, then a leading activist

27. Kelvin Charman on the crux of Botany Bay, HVS, 5a, at Subluminal Cliff, Swanage; a route made artificially difficult because of the problem of having to place vital protection while engaged on the crux moves

28. The chimney crack of Octo HVS 5a, on East Gully Wall was first climbed by Joe Brown in 1952. The wall to the left is taken by Ron Fawcett's Psycho Killer E6 6b

29. Ramshaw Rocks is best described as overhanging gritstone, its cracks and problems calling for extensive use of heel hooking, palming and jamming techniques. On the lower tier many of the routes have problematical starts; here, Paul Cornforth is on one of the harder introductory starts of Prostration HVS 5a

30. Lynn Rogers clipping the peg on Fratricide Wall HVS 5a, after which a step right – the crux – leads to the arête where the difficulties ease

31. In 1946 Peter Harding added a direct finish to Cave Innominate at Stanage at HVS 5a. This well-protected roof crack provides an excellent finish to a fine gritstone classic

32. Ian Parsons in mid-flight enjoying the final move on Promontory Nose HVS 5b. It is one of the advantages of climbing well within one's limits that such carefree moves can be made quite safely

33. Craig y Forwen is situated just north of Llangollen at the beauty spot of Worlds End. There are plenty of climbs at all grades though they are mainly short. Going Bad HVS 5B, is one of the more exposed climbs on the highest of the three tiers

34. Choe Brooks performing gymnastics on Chequers Buttress HVS 5b. Late evening soloing is very popular among Peak District climbers at the Edges of Froggatt and Burbage. The Chequers Buttress and Valkyrie HVS 5a at Froggatt are two of the most enjoyable and exposed gritstone solos: they hold no hidden terrors and there are good grips all the way

35. The Wilton Quarries on the outskirts of Bolton in Lancashire offer excellent short routes. Dawn HVS 5b was first climbed in 1963 by Rowland Edwards and is the classic for its grade at the crag. To the left is Christine Arête E3 5c, often soloed, though only by the bold and talented

36. Bird Rock is near Dolgellau in North Wales and situated away from the popular climbing areas. It is infrequently visited because of its distance from the major roads but the quality of climbing is excellent. Mick Brothers is on the top pitch of The Bolero HVS 5b, first climbed in 1974 by John Sumner, a very prominent mid-Wales activist

37. Mark Edwards on the crux of Rock Dancer E1 5a. The move involves a mantelshelf to reach a one finger pocket. The route is characteristic of the excellent open face climbing found on this superb slab of rock, which appears to be totally holdless when viewed from a distance but, in fact, is full of small holds

38. Leopard's Crawl E1 5b, was first climbed by Jim

183

Birkett in 1947, and is here being soloed by Al Phizacklea. Dow Crag is one of the Lake District's best and largest cliffs, and boasts superb classics of all standards

39. Andy Hyslop in fading evening light, running up the final section of Gimmer String E1 5b. This route was first climbed in 1963 by a formidable party consisting of Eric Metcalfe, D. Miller, and the leader J. Allan Austin. Gimmer Crag is perhaps the most famous climbing ground in Langdale with routes such as Kipling Groove, The Crack and Eastern Hammer. The quality of the rock provides excellent grips and plentiful protection

40. Keith Robertson starting off up North West Passage E1 5b, one of the many routes climbed by Jim Moran in 1978, an important year for Gogarth exploration

41. Ian Fox cutting loose on the lip of Mojo E1 5b. The route was first climbed by Rowland Edwards in 1959 and heralded major developments on North Wales limestone. Craig y Forwyn is in the rain shadow of Snowdonia and therefore remains very dry by comparison. This has encouraged thorough development of the crag which now boasts many classics both hard and easy

42. Bob Smith on the crux moves of Overhanging Crack E1 5c at Bowden Doors. This excellent sandstone crag is exposed enough to stay dry in winter and provides a wealth of classic routes of all standards for climbers in Northumberland

43. American Dream, E1 5b, first climbed by Rowland Edwards in March 1980. One of Britain's foremost sea cliff activists, Edwards has produced many fine climbs on sea cliffs outside the usual areas of activity. Here he is climbing Zawn Kellys, a crag boasting excellent climbing on superb rock in tranquil surroundings

44. Satan's Slip, E2 5a, is surely the best slab climb in Britain. Protection is sparse and it is best tackled solo on sight to obtain the fullest effect of the surroundings. The first half consists of 4b moves and leads the climber to the central break; from here the final 200 feet is very sustained 5a slab climbing with no resting points. The slab itself is one of Britain's finest natural land forms

45. Lord of the Rings E2 5b is the girdle traverse on the East Buttress of Scafell and is some 1500 feet in length. The route was first climbed by John Adams and Colin Read. It provides several hours of climbing on this magnificent high mountain crag usually going from left to right

46. The Tool was first climbed with aid in 1974 and free climbed by George Hounsome in 1978 at E2 5b. Here Graeme Allen is in the exposed bottomless groove below the final head wall. The crashing waves below and the instability of the rock at the ruckle make it a very enjoyable and entertaining climb

47. The Falcon Crags of Borrowdale overlook Derwent Water and Keswick. Rob Knight is on Fawcett's The Dangler E2 5b. Borrowdale, one of the Lake District's most picturesque areas, abounds in excellent climbing cliffs such as Goat Crag, Black Crag, Shepherd's Crag and Bowderstone Crag

48. Lydia Bradey on the final pitch of Exterminating Angel E2 5b. The sea walls and the main wall at Avon have quite a few bits of loose rock and the routes can be terrifying experiences. Protection in most cases consists of in situ pegs, some less than reliable. However, this all adds spice to the climbing on this group of crags near an urban area

49. Devotee E2 5c was first climbed by Ben and Marion Wintringham in 1979. The route takes a direct line through the classic route Gogarth HVS 5b, starting up the arête on the Gogarth Pinnacle as in the photo, and a fairly direct line to continue in a superb position

50. John Hartley ponders the problems presented by Brazen Buttress E2 5b. This single pitch 120 feet climb, first climbed in 1976 by Pat Littlejohn, was one of the first and best routes on Mother Carey's Kitchen. Littlejohn had a hand in climbing most of the hard routes on this cliff and indeed most others in South Pembroke

51. Brainbiter E2 5c, a magnificently-positioned climb overlooking the lower gorge and the town of Cheddar beyond

52. Paul Williams high up on Jabberwocky E2 5c, negotiating the crux moves. Although famed for the quality of its climbing, it is also very enjoyable for sunbathing and swimming at the foot of this crag beside one of Wales's peaceful and secluded llyns

53. Crumpet Crack at Helsby E2 5c, was first climbed in 1958 by Hugh Banner. The climbing is easy under the roof with good jams at the lip. From there it becomes increasingly awkward to continue and is made even more awkward by a supply of green moss on the rock. Here Gaz Healey is soloing the route with nonchalant ease on a fine August evening

54. Steve Lewis, major South Wales activist, on the crux moves of Grande Plage, E2 6a, Easter 1983. The Cornish sea cliffs enjoy better than average weather for this time of year and attract leading climbers from all over the country

55. Insanity E3 5c. Chris Nicholson savouring the delights of this awkward climb. The route was the object of many jamming attempts by Whillans and Brown, until in 1958 Hugh Banner tried laybacking and succeeded. He returned to lead it with Brown, Whillans and others and was very relieved when he completed the ascent in a single push

56. Craig Pant Ifan is high above the road and has many slabs and arête climbs. Paul Cropper, obviously very relaxed, is enjoying the slab section of Silly Arête E3 6a

57. Pete Livesey on home territory in 1983, tackling the crux of the first pitch of Mulatto Wall E3 5c. Malham Cove was previously an aid climbers' domain but free climbing has taken precedence with many excellent routes on the wings of the Cove

58. Controlled Burning, E3 5c. The route is aptly named since controlled effort is needed to avoid

'burning out' before the hard, final section. Here Gibson, the first ascensionist, is pulling round the overhang and approaching these crux moves. It is the finest route of its type on Lundy, requiring moves similar to those found on many crack climbs in the United States and it has an unrivalled situation

59. Steve Findlay approaching the crux of Arms Race, E3 5c, very aptly named by Steve Monks in 1979 due to the strenuousness of the climb. The character of all the routes on the Unknown Walls is similar in this respect, providing steep, well protected climbing five minutes from Bristol city centre

60. Alun Richardson on the crux of Finger Print E3 6a which was originally climbed by Andy Sharp with one point of aid and later freed by Pat Littlejohn. Ogmore in general is vertical or steeper and therefore offers plenty of climbing in the HVS and upwards bracket on good sound rock. The easier climbs are fewer but still worthwhile, the corner to the left, Pluto VS, a fine example

61. Quietus E3 6a, first climbed by Joe Brown in 1956, then a major step forward in climbing standards. Here Mark Stokes is on the right-hand variation, making very exposed moves which require faultless hand jamming techniques to succeed

62. Richard 'Nipper' Harrison on the crux of Pleasure Dome E3 5c, at Pembroke. This single pitch, classic E3 was first climbed by Pat Littlejohn in 1980 along an obvious line of weakness. Ron Fawcett climbed a direct line up the face called Stennis the Menace E6 6b which starts on its right and finishes in the crackline to the left of Nipper

63. Hole of Creation E3 6a, first climbed by Paul Williams in 1983. Andy Newton abseils down the route to remove the gear of a previous ascent. The difficulties are easy to see: overhanging rock make awkward pendulums in mid-air

64. Pete O'Donovan cutting loose on the direct finish of Kingdom Come E3 6a, at Stoney Middleton. The crux of the climb is the first few moves. However, its position on Windy Buttress makes the remainder steep and exposed and it is one of Stoney's most exhilarating routes

65. High Performance was first climbed with aid in 1960 by G. and R. Farquhar and named Coffin Arête. In 1978 Dave Cuthbertson free climbed the route with little trouble to provide an excellent, gymnastic E3 6a, on this roadside crag

66. No Red Tape E3 6a, first climbed by Gary and Phil Gibson in 1983 was aptly named, as most of Gary's new routes on Pen Trwyn had in situ red tape threads. The bolt being meanly placed, so that a dangerous fall was still possible before clipping the bolt. The actual crux move, demonstrated here by Malcolm Campbell, is just above the bolt and quite entertaining

67. This spectacular shot was taken from a tyrolean traverse set up between the two arêtes of the Cromlech, using an 8mm fisheye lens. The two walls give perhaps the best wall climbing in Britain: some routes follow cracks while others take sequences of

pockets. The grades average out at E4 6a, and they were first climbed by Joe Brown, Don Whillans, Steve Wunsch, Pete Livesey, Ron Fawcett, John Redhead, and the author

68. Here the belayer can afford to relax and sunbathe for Ian Jones is steaming up the crux moves of Stroll On E4 6a, first climbed by Ron Fawcett and Pete Livesey in 1976 as a direct finish to Roll On E3 5c. The Grochan has plenty of climbs similar to this steep, sustained one which are often very technical for the grade. Climbing here usually consists of sequences using side pulls, on soapy textured rock

69. The Knock was first climbed in 1975 by John Allen at E4 5c. Now repeating the route he is approaching the difficult and serious final section. The climb is typical of many short gritstone routes where there is just enough height to make the climber feel vulnerable and add some spice

70. The Axe E4 6a, first climbed in 1979 by Pat Littlejohn, must be one of Britain's most exposed climbs. Here Martin Crook is completing the crux moves on the single 160 foot pitch. Cloggy faces north and stands 2500 feet above sea level, so it takes awhile for the cliff to dry out sufficiently for these routes to be enjoyed

71. George Smith on the crux moves of Top Gear E4 6a at Threshwaite Cove. The climb was the scene of a serious accident when Pete Whillance fell from a damp patch near the top: he was saved by a runner only feet from the ground but still bounced due to his rope stretching. He later returned to lead it and claim the first ascent

72. Spider Mackenzie on The Führer E4 5c, a very serious route. When standing at the foot of the cliff, the height is deceptively low but it quickly becomes obvious when you embark on the climb and begin to sample its sustained and severe difficulties. Surprisingly, the rock is almost identical to Castell Helen on Gogarth

73. Sultans of Swing E4 6a, though not the hardest route on the Vector Headwall, is most probably the best. The final 140-foot pitch offers superb climbing on sound and well-protected rock at this popular, low lying crag

74. Mark Leach on the crux moves of Pigs on the Wing E4 6b, at Wilton 2. This bouldering-type route is typical of the harder climbs in the quarries, needing accurate footwork and very strong fingers. It was first climbed by John Hartley, who used a side runner, but it was soloed at a later date by Charlton Chestwig

75. The slate quarries of North Wales normally offer little high quality climbing. However, Vivian Quarry at Llanberis has two brilliant lines: Comes the Dervish E5 6a first climbed by Stevie Haston (and pictured here); and Andy Pollitt's Flashdance E6 6a, which starts 30 feet to the right and leads up to the climber's position here

76. Matt Boyer on Axle Attack on Pen Trwyn. This was originally attempted as a bolt route but the ascent was abandoned halfway up. Mel Griffiths and Leigh McGinley added three more bolts, then free climbed

the entire line which has now become the classic E5 6a of the crag. Pen Trwyn, within minutes of Llandudno, has a very high concentration of extreme limestone climbs: it is a climbers' paradise and blessed with good weather

77. Steve Lewis in mid-air after falling out of the crack on Behemoth E5 6a. Originally climbed by Ron Fawcett and Pete Livesey, it has undergone many changes since as holds have come off due to the looseness of the rock. The final crack, however, remains as flared and frictionless as ever and defeats many aspiring leaders. Falling off steep limestone is relatively safe as you fall well clear of the rock making chances of injury slight

78. Daniel Lee on the top section of Coventry Street E5 6a. Originally climbed in two pitches by John Allen and Steve Bancroft, it is now often led in one. A thin finger crack with a crux move at the top is necessary to gain entry to the cave. Sandy grovelling leads to the lip and the main crux, pulling on to the headwall follows

79. Infidel at High Rocks 6b, not soloed, first climbed by Mick Fowler in 1978. Here Guy Mclelland is using the undercut to reach the first break, after which a mantleshelf and a one-arm pull-through are needed to reach the top. The antique inscription to the right reflects its history – it used to be a pleasure park – and remains a tranquil and delightful spot

80. The Main Cliff at Gogarth, perhaps Britain's finest sea cliff, is a 300-foot high wall with plenty of steep, well protected climbs of E5 and E6. Approach along its foot is possible at low tide only, and climbers are sometimes left with just the option of climbing out, and the easiest escape route is an E4 5c. Here Mark Lynden is climbing the second pitch of Hunger E5 6b 6a, pioneered by Pat Littlejohn in 1978

81. The North York Moors was a climbing area removed from the mainstream of development until the 1980s, with the exception of some climbing by John Readhead in the 1970s. After the addition of many hard routes their potential was recognised. Here Nick Dixon is completing the crux section of Magic in the Air E5 6b, made only just safe with the preplaced runner by abseil down to his right, warranted by the brittleness of the rock

82. The previously undiscovered Hodge Close Quarry began to be developed in 1980. It is the only slate crag of any significance in the Lakes. Ed Cleasby, South Lakes superstar, is captured here cruising on Pete Whillance's Life in the Fast Lane E5 6a. This route, The Main Event E5 6a, and Stage Fright E5 6b, 30 yards to the left, are the crag's desperates. Climbing here is for the cool-headed only and some consider it dangerous as most of the routes are sparsely protected and the rock brittle

83. Tales of Yankee Power, first climbed by Phil Burke in 1979 at E5 6b. This climb is typical of routes on High Tor: low friction rock with small pocket holds and requiring great strength and stamina from fingers and toes. Here Phil Burke is on the technical crux at the beginning of the main difficulties, which are sustained with few rest ledges

84. Pete Whillance in a crucifix position on the crux of his own climb Incantations E5 6b. The Napes cliffs, overlooking Wasdale, are in one of the most impressive positions in the Lake District. The modern classics The Vikings E3 to the left and Supernatural E4 to the right are also found on this wall

85. Giant Killer E6 6a, a 20 foot ceiling at Dinas Rock, first climbed by Pat Littlejohn in 1983. A few hard moves lead to the roof where the difficulties begin after a 'committing' move on to the ceiling; a curving crack leads to the lip and placing protection is very strenuous. The lip reached, one can rest if necessary, and then hard moves lead up to a belay. The second pitch still overhangs some 15 degrees and follows an interesting series of grooves to the right of the free hanging ivy

86. The Golden Mile was first climbed in 1980 by Pete Livesey and his brother at E5 6a. However, over the past few years various holds have fallen off and it is now rated E6 6b. This 160 feet, single pitch climb starts with some easy moves up the wall after which the climbing rapidly becomes harder up to the technical crux gaining the rest ledge where the climber soon finds that the 'rest ledge' is nothing of the kind. A continuous series of hard and often blind moves then lead to the top. Chris Hamper is seen steaming away from the ledge in the intense heat of an afternoon in July

87. Paradise Lost E6 6b 6b. Steve Monks is seen here on the second pitch at sunset, bridging up the crux clipping protection. The climb, first done as an aid route, had its aid reduced to a single point by Pete Livesey. Subsequent ascents by Ron Fawcett, Monks, Nipper Harrison, Pat Littlejohn and Pete O'Donovan have also required a single point of aid, but a different one in each case. Martin Crocker climbed it in one push in 1984. Rusty bolts make this the most serious undertaking in Cheddar

88. Gary Latter on the crux moves of Cosmopolitan E5 6c. This overhanging crackline was first climbed by Dave Cuthbertson in 1982 and heralded the introduction of technically very hard climbing to the Glen Nevis area. The ascent was prepared the previous day with inspections and gardening sessions by abseil: a precedent that has influenced high-grade climbing in Scotland

89. Quentin Fisher soloing Piranha E6 6c. The whole of the Rubicon Wall offers very technical climbing on small holds with adequate protection only. It was developed mainly by Ron Fawcett, Dominic and Daniel Lee, and now provides some standard tests for high-grade climbers

90. The author, solo, approaching the crux of Tobacco Road 6c at Bowles Rocks. I made the first ascent with Guy Mclelland in 1982 after many assaults on the wall's other routes. It starts with a 'sequence' hand traverse leading left, then goes straight up the wall before breaking off to the right around the main overhang where the crux moves bear right and up

91. Joe Healey soloing the classic Black Magic E6 6a, at Pex Hill Quarry. The route involves very sustained 6a climbing and is highly serious. Seriousness is not

usual at Pex Hill, which is one of Britain's foremost bouldering crags, offering many problems of all grades to 7a. Black Magic was first soloed in 1979 by Phil Davidson, the most prominent local activist

92. Bloodstone E6 6b, was first climbed in 1983 by Simon Nadin. The route is typical of the harder routes at the Roches: delicate, fingery slabs often in serious positions. The crack behind is taken by the Mincer HVS, with another route, Smear Test E2 6a, following the crack then traversing across the slab to the nearside crack. Bloodstone's totally direct line up the centre of the slab is protectionless after the difficulties start, and is quite dangerous!

93. Roadrunner E6 6c. First climbed by Ron Fawcett in 1981, it is unusually serious by High Tor standards. Andy Pollitt is just about to clip into the peg: this position is regarded as the completion of the crux moves. Climbs of this severity and seriousness are often tackled quickly, the abandonment of gear being of little consequence to the merits of falling off

94. For hard limestone climbing, Raven Tor is the best climbing cliff in the Peak District. It overhangs dramatically giving very steep, sustained climbing and even in heavy rain the routes remain dry. Here Dominic Lee is approaching the first break on the first pitch of Ron Fawcett's Indecent Exposure E6 6c 6b. At the second break the route escapes to the right. Fawcett's nearby The Prow, E7 6c 6c 7a, finishes straight up the main prow

95. Tiger Mountain E7 6b previously known as Cave Route and originally an A3 aid climb. On one of Pete Livesey's early attempts at freeing the route he stopped himself from falling by lunging for an aid climber's rope, much to the latter's surprise. Some time later it was free climbed by Ron Fawcett. Phil Davidson tackles the crux, having just climbed 110 feet of unrelenting 6a moves

96. Adrenalin Rush 7b was first climbed by Allan Manson. It is best described as a BIG boulder problem. The first half is easy, but the second becomes increasingly difficult and is full of hidden obstacles. At 35 feet the top is almost within reach but the bottom is climbers' more usual destination. Very few, however, proceed far enough to test their ability to bounce harmlessly

97. The Great White, E7 6c, takes the main crackline on the mirror-smooth face of the White Tower, and was first climbed by Ron Fawcett in 1982. Here Mick Lovatt approaches the crux section, where the crack runs out and face dinks are used to ascend further. Because the sea cliffs are constantly sprayed with water, the chalk stays on the crag for a very short period of time only. This presents subsequent leaders with route-finding problems not found on many inland crags which remain permanently chalked up

98. In 1983 Dumbarton Rock was the scene of the ascent of Requiem E7 7a, by Dave Cuthbertson. Although not ascended in pure style with many yo-yos and ropes left in place, it was completed to give Scotland's hardest route. Because it is a crack climb runners have to be placed during the ascent which makes the route even more strenuous than its

appearance suggests. On most hard limestone routes the bolts and pegs would be *in situ*, quick and easy to clip, and even on the first ascent two nuts were placed by abseil prior to ascent

99. Little Plum at Stoney Middleton, previously an A3 aid route, now climbed free at E7 7a 6c by Jerry Moffatt. The first pitch is highly technical and uses small holds leading to a hanging belay; it was first climbed in 1981. The second pitch, overhanging and strenuous, was climbed in 1982 thus completing the climb

100. John Redhead on The Bells, The Bells E7 6b, which he first climbed in 1980. This is the most serious rock climb in Britain, consisting of steep, sustained, 6b climbing – loose and friable rock without protection. The wall to the left has two much easier climbs, Fawcett's The Cad E5 6a and Pete Whillance's The Long Run E6 6a. The guidebook describes Redhead's route as 'a lonely soul-searching lead which needs total commitment'

◼ GLOSSARY ◼

Abseil (rappel): A quick method of descent by sliding down the rope using a purpose-designed friction device

Aid: Climbing which relies on artificial aids such as pitons, expansion bolts and chockstones to overcome a problem

Activist: A climber responsible for significant achievements

Arête: In climbing, an arête is an outhrust prow of rock

Ascenders (cloggers): Gadgets which are pushed up a rope until they jam and then the climber pulls himself up the rope holding onto slings dangling from them

Belay: An anchoring device to safeguard the rest of a climbing party if one of them falls (see runners)

Boulder problem: An exceptionally difficult move

B1: A boulder problem

B2: A boulder problem repeated only by its inventor

B3: An unrepeated boulder problem

Betterbrake: Device used for abseiling and belaying

Bolts (expansion bolts): A hole is drilled in the rockface and an expansion bolt, containing a bracket to which a karabiner can be attached, is screwed into it.

Buttress: A large projection of rock on a mountain side

Bold: An exposed and poorly protected piece of climbing

Backing off: Retreating from a bold section

Bulge: A projecting boss of rock

Cruise: A smooth and trouble-free ascent

Choss: Loose and unreliable rock

Classic: A popular and famous climb

Crux: The hardest part of the climb

Ceiling: A flat roof overhang

Corner: The conjunction of two faces of rock when set approximately at right angles

Dangle and whack merchant: An aid climber

Descendeur: See Figure-of-eight

Dinks: Extremely small holds

Dièdre: A large corner or groove in a crag similar to that of an open book

Dead hang: Hanging from one's hands

EB: Trade name for a rock boot popular in the 1970s

Ethics: The conventions governing rock climbing

Expansion bolts: See Bolts

Exposure: The psychological effect of finding oneself high above the ground in an exposed position

Epic: When things don't go quite right

Friends: Protection devices (see gear chapter)

Frigging: Employing aid on a free climb

Figure-of-eight: An abseiling device

Flake: A partly detached, flattish leaf of rock

Free climbing: Climbing without resorting to the use of artificial aids

Finger board: A training aid used for practising pull-ups

Grade: Reflects the difficulty of climb

Gardening: Preparation of a climb prior to ascent: removal of loose material, vegetation

Groove: A shallow, vertical depression in the rock

Guidebook: Detailed list of climbs for a given area

Gullies: Steep-sided watercourses found on rocky mountain sides

Girdle traverse: A traverse which goes from one side of a crag to another instead of from bottom to top

Gripped: An attack of nerves while climbing

Hand traverse: Performing a traverse without the benefit of footholds

Ironmongery: Equipment used for aid climbing

Jamming: Jamming one's feet and hands in a fissure in the rockface to form a friction hold

Jug: A very large incut hold

Karabiner (Krab): D-shaped metal link usually made from aluminium alloy

Kernmantel: Modern climbing rope consisting of a central core, Kern (for strength), and a protective mantle

Leading: Going up a pitch first when in a roped party

Layback: A difficult technique used for climbing cracks; feet are placed against the protruding edge and hands grip nearer edge thus working them in opposition. Hands and feet are then moved in sequence

Layaway: Using a side hold while climbing

Mank: see Choss

Mantleshelf: A move on rock similar to that of getting out of a swimming pool and used to overcome a very high step

Nut: A wedge-shaped piece of metal jammed into a crack on a rockface to which a runner can be attached

Nut tool: Small blade-shaped piece of metal used to remove jammed nuts

On sight ascent: To climb a route without any prior knowledge of it

Overhang: Overhanging piece or section of rock

PA: Trade name for the first-ever design of rock boot

Peg (piton): Metal spike with eyelet hole, hammered into cracks in the rockface

Protection: Any device which is attached to the rockface to stop a climber falling and usually arranged by a leader e.g. runners

Pitch: The section between belay points

Problem: A technically difficult move requiring a great deal of prior consideration

Runner: A runner consists of a tape sling hung over a jutting piece of rock or threaded around a chockstone. The sling is then clipped on to a karabiner which is attached to the main climbing rope. By using this protective device the maximum a climber can fall is twice the distance between him and the runner

RP: Very small brass nut

Run out: Term used to describe the distance between a climber and his last runner placement or belay point

Roof: The underside of a large overhang

Route: Specific way up a rockface

Rack: A climber's collection of protection devices

Rocks: Stoppers/chockstones with convex and concave faces

Straights: Stoppers/chockstones with flat faces

Stoppers: Wedge-shaped nuts threaded on to wire or rope

Seconding: Going second up a pitch when in a roped party

Sticht plate: The first-ever type of mechanical belaying device invented by Fritz Sticht. Instead of the rope passing round the climber's back, it passes through a metal friction plate which applies a gradual brake to the rope if another climber falls

Sharp end, the: Leading

Skyhook: Metal hook used for lowering off when the leader fails on a pitch

Slab: A flat face of rock set at an angle less than vertical, usually between 30 and 75 degrees

Stance: The top of a pitch and usually a ledge

Stemming: Bridging across a groove or corner

Steep rock: Vertical or overhanging

Serious: A climb where the consequences of a fall would inevitably be grave

Tape: Strong nylon webbing especially made for climbing

Thin: A section of climbing using very small holds

Top roping: A rope held from above and used for short climbs, inspection of a new climb or difficult pitch or a leader in difficulty

Traversing: Making moves to the left or right rather than up

Trog up: To walk up to a high level crag

Wire brush: Used by climbers to clean holds

Way off: The most convenient descent route from a cliff top

Whizzer: A dramatic 'Fast Fall'

Zawn: A deep sea inlet surrounded by cliffs

━INDEX━